The Power of Agency

Other Books by
Frederick A. Miller and Judith H. Katz

*Change Champions: A Dialogic Approach
to Creating an Inclusive Culture*
(BMI, 2022) (Frederick A. Miller, Monica E. Biggs,
and Judith H. Katz)

*Safe Enough to Soar: Accelerating Trust, Inclusion &
Collaboration in the Workplace*
(Berrett-Koehler, 2018)

*Opening Doors to Teamwork and Collaboration: 4 Keys
That Change Everything*
(Berrett-Koehler, 2013)

Be BIG: Step Up, Step Out, Be Bold
(Berrett-Koehler, 2008)

*The Inclusion Breakthrough: Unleashing
the Real Power of Diversity*
(Berrett-Koehler, 2002)

*The Promise of Diversity: Over 40 Voices Discuss
Strategies for Eliminating Discrimination in
Organizations*
(Irwin/NTL, 1994) (Elsie Y. Cross, Judith H. Katz,
Frederick A. Miller, and Edie W. Seashore, Eds.)

Other Books by
Judith H. Katz

White Awareness: Handbook for Anti-Racism Training
(University of Oklahoma Press, 1978, 2003)

*No Fairy Godmothers, No Magic Wands:
The Healing Process after Rape*
(R&E Publishers, 1984)

THE
POWER OF
AGENCY

Cultivating Autonomy, Authority, and Leadership in Every Role

FREDERICK A. MILLER & JUDITH H. KATZ

Berrett–Koehler Publishers, Inc.

Berrett-Koehler Publishers, Inc.
1333 Broadway, Suite P100
Oakland, CA 94612–1921
Tel: (510) 817–2277
Fax: (510) 817–2278
bkconnection.com

ORDERING INFORMATION
Quantity sales. Special discounts are available on quantity purchases by corporations, associations, and others. For details, please go to bkconnection.com to see our bulk discounts or contact bookorders@bkpub.com for more information.
Individual sales. Berrett-Koehler publications are available through most bookstores. They can also be ordered directly from Berrett-Koehler: Tel: (800) 929–2929; Fax: (802) 864–7626; bkconnection.com.
Orders for college textbook / course adoption use. Please contact Berrett-Koehler: Tel: (800) 929–2929; Fax: (802) 864–7626.

Distributed to the US trade and internationally by Penguin Random House Publisher Services.

Berrett-Koehler and the BK logo are registered trademarks of Berrett-Koehler Publishers, Inc.

Printed in the United States of America

Berrett-Koehler books are printed on long-lasting, acid-free paper. When it is available, we choose paper that has been manufactured by environmentally responsible processes. These may include using trees grown in sustainable forests, incorporating recycled paper, minimizing chlorine in bleaching, or recycling the energy produced at the paper mill.

Library of Congress Cataloging-in-Publication Data

Names: Miller, Frederick A., 1946- author. | Katz, Judy H., 1950- author.
Title: The power of agency : cultivating autonomy, authority, and leadership in every role / Frederick A. Miller, Judith H. Katz.
Description: First edition. | Oakland, CA : Berrett-Koehler Publishers, Inc., [2025] | Includes bibliographical references and index.
Identifiers: LCCN 2024019318 (print) | LCCN 2024019319 (ebook) | ISBN 9798890570352 (paperback) | ISBN 9798890570369 (pdf) | ISBN 9798890570376 (epub)
Subjects: LCSH: Work—Psychological aspects. | Autonomy (Psychology) | Work environment—Psychological aspects. | Employees—Attitudes. | Organizational behavior. | Teams in the workplace. | Leadership.
Classification: LCC HF5548.8 .M4923 2025 (print) | LCC HF5548.8 (ebook) | DDC 158.7—dc23/eng/20240710
LC record available at https://lccn.loc.gov/2024019318
LC ebook record available at https://lccn.loc.gov/2024019319

First Edition
32 31 30 29 28 27 26 25 24   10 9 8 7 6 5 4 3 2 1

Book production: Westchester Publishing Services
Cover design: Amoreena O'Bryon

We dedicate this book to the people who have toiled under the challenges of workplaces where they were not fully valued, where they did not receive all the thanks and rewards that they deserved. To the people who had more to give, and more thoughts for improvement to share. And all the people who have made the progress of the twenty-first century possible and, if fully unleashed with agency, will make this an even better century for human advancement. There is much work to do, and we know that we humans can do it. We celebrate our journey to even higher heights.

Fred   *Judith*

Contents

Foreword

by Christopher Del Vecchio
President and CEO, MVP Health Care

The journey to understand that agency and meaningful work are core to our humanity has slowly unfolded since the founding of the United States. Historically, progress was selective, safeguarding the status quo. Yet, today stands as a testament to our collective learning curve, embracing the wisdom of our past, both its triumphs and trials. Now, a substantial part of our team consists of knowledge workers, pioneers in innovation and agents of change through their forward-thinking ideas. At MVP, we celebrate this transformative era, pledging to always honor the progress of our history while nurturing the contributions of every mind in our community.

At MVP, innovation isn't just a buzzword for us—it's a guiding principle that propels us forward. We are driven by a desire to discover new ways of doing things to improve how we serve our customers and our communities. And that's precisely why I am thrilled to pen this foreword for *The Power of Agency* by Frederick A. Miller and Judith H. Katz.

This captivating book delves deep into the concept of agency, emphasizing the importance of autonomy, leadership, and authority in every role. It provides individuals, team members, and leaders with a powerful framework to assess and enrich their levels of agency. But *The Power of Agency* goes beyond individual growth—it is a testament to our collective journey toward creating workplaces that foster success.

As I read through this thought-provoking book, I couldn't help but reflect on the values and principles that have embodied my professional journey. Throughout my career, I have grown to deeply understand the critical importance of fostering workplace cultures that embrace agency. Without it, individuals struggle to forge meaningful connections to their work, leading to a stifling of creativity, passion, and a diminished sense of accountability. We recognize the hunger for agency among individuals who yearn to contribute and propel organizations forward. If organizations fail to nurture agency, they risk losing top talent to competitors who can harness the full potential of their employees.

In this book, the authors aptly describe the importance of ensuring that all individuals, regardless of their roles, levels, tenure, and identities, have the power, influence, and voice to make choices and decisions in their jobs for the betterment of our organizations.

At MVP, we know that true agency goes beyond simply having the latitude to do your job or making decisions without parameters. It is about taking owner-ship of your work, being accountable for your actions, and embracing the opportunities to learn and grow. It is about collaborating with others, communicating openly, and making decisions with the support and knowledge of those around you.

We also recognize that agency is not possible if you don't have a leadership team encouraging and build-ing safe spaces. Building an organization that supports and promotes the progress of agency is a journey, not a destination. MVP is not striving for perfection but for continuous improvement. We embrace the chal-lenges and opportunities that arise, always seeking new ways to better serve our customers and team members. We understand that growth and change re-quire humility, a willingness to learn from our expe-riences, and the courage to adapt and evolve.

As a leader in the health care industry, I am acutely aware that promoting and providing agency isn't al-ways a straightforward task. It requires us to challenge our natural inclination to maintain control. However, by following the insightful guidelines put forth by Fred and Judith, your organization will witness first-hand the immense benefits of embracing the fact that brilliant ideas can come from anyone within the team when you strive to create an environment that encour-ages everyone to contribute their unique perspectives. By acknowledging and promoting agency within your organization, you will not only empower your employees, but also cultivate a culture of continuous improvement.

Together, let us embrace the power of agency and unlock the limitless potential within organizations. *The Power of Agency* is an inspiration for those who value innovation and progress. It reminds us that agency is not just a leadership trait but a human condition, residing deep within our souls. It calls on us to embrace change and actively contribute to building an agency-driven culture.

I invite you to dig into the pages of this noteworthy book and discover the power of agency for yourself. Let us embark on this journey of personal and professional growth together, as we strive to create a future where agency is not just a buzzword but a way of life.

Thank you, Fred and Judith, for generously sharing your profound wisdom and invaluable insights. The quote by Antoine de Saint-Exupéry, "If you want to build a ship, don't drum up people to gather wood, divide the work, and give orders. Instead, teach them to yearn for the vast and endless sea," beautifully encapsulates the transformative power of agency that resides within each of us.

Foreword

**by Dr. Yabome Gilpin-Jackson
First Vice-President, People, Equity,
and Inclusion at Simon Fraser
University**

The essence of agency is that it is self-motivated and self-directed. When we invite agency, we are evoking personal choice because of, and sometimes in spite of, the internal and external discourses and circumstances we face. Agency can be cultivated and encouraged through our upbringing, education, and in the workplace, through leadership and organizational structures. However, even when conditions for agency are in place, the decision to exercise agency is self-motivated—and therein lies its challenge and complexity. Agency is influenced both by external and internal processes. Individuals need to exercise agency as actors who shape their own futures as well as large-scale change; transformations are only successful when collective agentic action is undertaken at every level. Individuals and teams must choose agency. It is for this reason top-down, authoritarian, and bureaucratic approaches to management and leadership often fail.

This book aims to unleash the agency of everyone in organizations as part of a call for radical inclusion. It provides strategies and tools for cultivating the autonomy, authority, and leadership of everyone in organizations, regardless of their personhood or role. As a leader, organization development scholar, and consultant, I have experienced and learned many of the lessons the authors have codified in this book. I understand the crucial nature of the ten steps to unleash agency in organizations (see Figure P2.1), as it models the core principles of dialogic organization development. In addition, this book reiterates the need for culture change across an entire organization and addresses the power of agency at the individual, team, and system-wide levels within it.

Agency Is Core to Individual Leadership Development

As the authors show in Chapters 8 and 10, agency is inherent to each person's inner capability and, to be fully unleashed, it must be supported through management practices and organizational conditions. Throughout my career, I have seen the fundamental difference agency makes when leaders build their capacity and muscle to support the individuals they lead in exercising agency for the organization's betterment. They understand that one of the best things they can do is to cultivate an informal network of leaders and change champions who take responsibility for an organization's challenges and opportunities. Key findings from a case study review and research study I conducted on a large-scale organization development initiative showed that having formal leaders participate as champions in the change process was a core contextual condition to creating a transformational change experience.[1] The study also showed that the realization of leadership potential—and ultimately increased agency—was a clear outcome, one that advanced participants' professional career success.

Agency Supports Team and Organizational Development and Change

In Chapter 9, the authors explore how teams can embrace agency, summarizing conditions that support positive organization development and culture change through practices like dialogue, collective action, and collaboration. Time and again, management, organization development, and change research have provided evidence that change processes geared toward unleashing the collective agency and actions of those most impacted by change yield the most positive and sustainable results. These approaches involve dialogic organization development methodologies and mindsets that acknowledge the interconnectedness and socially constructed nature of organizational life, and rely on collective high-inquiry methods. These methods disrupt status quo narratives and allow for the emergence of new ones. A study has shown that nine out of ten change efforts that involve dialogic approaches are successful. In contrast, only about a third of the change and transformation processes that are initiated through traditional methodologies (which rely solely on objective, analytical, and planned approaches to change) are successful.[2] In their previous works, Fred Miller and Judith Katz, along with co-author Monica Biggs, have also used case examples to show that the dialogic organization development approach, supported by change champions, "accelerates, enhances, and dramatically increases the success of organizational culture change."[3] Most importantly, they show this approach creates inclusive cultures.

Agency Is at the Center of System-Wide and Social Change

Agency has always been at the center for those who resist the status quo in order to effect change within systems of oppression and marginality, from the women's movement, to employment equity, to racial justice. Through my work with equity-deserving and denied communities, whether in organizations or communities, I have found agency to be at the core of the transformative development of socially marginalized people, alongside identity formation and finding places of belonging. While self-identity formation (differentiation from harmful and negative social stereotypes) and a sense of belonging (finding anchoring and nourishing communities) are fundamental to the growth of individuals and communities in these circumstances, it is agency that makes the transformative difference to shifting negative narratives and creating change actions.

Organizations that take on the challenge of unleashing agency will be saying "yes" to fostering this deep form of development for people of all diversities, and will be working directly on building more inclusive workplace cultures. In turn, this will increase a sense of belonging and inclusion when it is clear that the power to act in accordance with the autonomy, authority, and leadership inherent in every organizational role is not reserved for a select few, based on markers of power and privilege. It means that such organizations will prioritize ensuring all organizational systems, as per the thoughts outlined in Chapter 12, are designed to unleash agency in everyone to do their best work.

To close, Anneli Eteläpelto and his co-authors suggest that, "If we wish to investigate professional agency in working life contexts, we need to understand how agency is practised, and how it is resourced, constrained, and bounded by contextual factors, including power relations and discourses, and further by the material conditions and cultures of social interaction in work communities."[4] That is what this book has accomplished and the promise that awaits those who take on the challenge of doing so.

Preface

This book represents the evolution of our thinking and work with people and organizations over the course of more than fifty years. Starting with our first book, *The Inclusion Breakthrough,* and in our subsequent books, we have written about how individuals and teams can Be BIG and how they can create environments in which people have the common language and inter-action safety needed to enhance collaboration, trust, and organization success. This has led us to this latest book on agency, which we see as the next step in indi-vidual, team, and organizational transformation.

> *Agency is ensuring that all people, of all roles, levels, ten-ure, and identities have the power, influence, and voice to make choices and decisions related to their jobs and the betterment of their organization.*

In this book we address how to unleash agency within organizations so that individuals, pairs, and teams can excel in their jobs, enhance their individ-ual and collective best work, and move to a higher level of performance within their roles. Unleashing agency at every level is key if everyone is to be able to contribute to the mission, vision, strategic priorities, and values of the organization—so that both individ-uals and the organization can soar.

At its core, this book aims to ensure everyone in the organization exercises agency, that everyone has the autonomy, authority, ownership, and decision-making capacity to take leadership in their work, and that everyone at every level can be the Operations Leader of their job. This book provides leaders with a detailed and practical process for creating a culture of agency in their organization. It also gives individuals, team members, managers, and leaders tools to assess their current level of agency and strategies to exercise greater agency as their organization operates in new ways to achieve higher performance.

While leveraging differences and inclusion are foundational to an organization's success, we believe that inclusion is not the end of the journey of change related to people and how they work together. We see agency as the next step on the path to creating even better organizations that outperform others, and workplaces that support people to do their best work and make their largest contribution!

For many in the workforce today, organizations and managers that make them feel small, smother them, limit their ability to contribute, and fail to value their talents, are no longer tolerable. Agency is key to retaining people and helping people, and helping an organization thrive.

Part I

How Agency Works in Organizations

At this stage of the twenty-first century, the world is an uncertain and changing place and the work environment reflects that uncertainty and change. Many people are now thinking about where and how work factors into their lives. They may have questions like the following:

Is this a place for me?

Is this a place where I want to spend the next days/months/years of my work-life energy?

Is this a place where I can have the work-life-me integration that I want and that will evolve?

Is this a place where I can grow and add to my portfolio of skills?

Is this a place where I am respected, valued, and seen for who I am?

Is this a place where I can contribute my talent and skills?

Is this a place where I can bring the knowledge and experience that I have?

Or

Do they treat me like a worker bee and fail to . . .

acknowledge my skills, talents, and know-how?

listen to me nor ask for my opinion?

give me flexibility and choice?

allow me to make decisions and act independently?

let me do the job I was hired to do?

only see me as an order-taker, a pair of hands and feet like in the factories of old, with little room to bring my thinking?

In the chapters that follow, we discuss the role that agency can play in your own and your organization's growth as we explore what agency is and is not; ways it can change organizations for the better by increasing efficiency, boosting morale, well-being, and performance; and, freeing up everyone at all levels to do their best work. We provide a step-by-step process to help you transform an organization's culture to one of greater agency. We also offer concrete guidance to assist you in unleashing agency for yourself and your team, for managers, supervisors, and leaders, through hands-on tools, strategies, and real-world examples. Change is not always easy, nor does it happen as quickly as we might like, so we will help you to troubleshoot by working through challenges and opportunities; finding new paths to higher individual, team, and organization performance; and enabling each person to do their best work. We are excited to invite you on this journey with us.

Chapter 1
A Case for Agency

The early morning meeting with the CEO and upper-level managers of the organization was a good one, and Jaime left feeling optimistic. She was glad she had come in today for this meeting, rather than attending virtually from home. She had been with the company for five years, was rated a high performer with high potential, and had recently started taking part in these strategy sessions. She appreciated being invited to the table and liked being able to see the big picture, which helped her better understand where her work fit in. As she made her way back to her desk, ideas for new projects bubbled in her mind. She was excited to bounce her thoughts off her team and try out some fresh initiatives. But, when she shared her ideas with one of her colleagues, he was not as excited. "There you go again being optimistic," he said. "You know what usually happens. They act positive in the meeting, and then later change their minds."

Jaime walked back to her desk and began writing an email to her manager, Kristina. But as she began to outline some of her ideas, she felt her energy fading. Even though she was Kristina's "right-hand person" and felt that Kristina valued her as a team member, this didn't translate into having the freedom to add value and implement her own thinking. When it came to taking action, Kristina treated Jaime like a junior member of the organization, someone who needed constant oversight and supervision. When Kristina did give Jaime tasks, or allow her to implement one of her own ideas, Jaime felt the strings that came along with it—the micromanagement, second-guessing of her actions, and required frequent check-ins that seemed more about easing Kristina's risk-averse mindset than about continuous improvement or coaching and mentoring. In short, Jaime felt smothered.

As she finished the email, Jaime sat back and stared at the words on the screen. She knew they were good ideas, but the optimism from the morning's meeting faded in the face of the reality of working at her organization. The more she thought about it, she realized her colleague was right, and that her ideas would go nowhere. She had been down this path before, and it was exhausting.

Kristina—with whom Jaime had a good relationship—still made sure every "i" was dotted, every "t" was crossed, and that every idea or project was dissected and discussed with her and others before it could even start to be implemented. Though Jaime knew Kristina's intentions were good, her comments instead felt controlling and smothering. This slowed Jaime down, undermined her, and stifled her creativity. Jaime felt as if she was just there to carry out instructions, to act more as a "doer" than someone with expertise who could truly add value to the organization. Sometimes she felt the organization was run by committee and lacked an intrapreneurial spirit which, in turn, negatively impacted its speed and competitiveness.

As Jaime leaned back in her chair, she felt the full weight of her frustration. What were all her education, skills, and experience with the organization worth if she couldn't work and contribute to the best of her ability? What was the point of her being there? Maybe she shouldn't put as much effort into her job and should spend more of her energy on life outside of work? Or maybe she should leave the organization altogether?

Over the next two weeks, Jaime continued to think about what had happened after the meeting and her past experiences while working there. As she reflected on each incident of feeling stifled and smothered by naysaying colleagues or being micromanaged, she thought more seriously about her career options. She reflected, "When I accepted this job, I had four other job offers—and two of those companies indicated I had an open offer. They really wanted me!" As much as she cared about the people in her current company, she had reached a momentous decision. It was time to move on. She decided to hand in her letter of resignation to Kristina.

Jaime Decides to Leave

Later that day, Jaime wasn't surprised when Kristina asked if they could meet. They went into Kristina's office and sat down.

"I wasn't expecting this." Kristina paused. "Can you tell me why you're leaving?"

Jaime hesitated. She wasn't sure how much to share.

"Is it the money?" asked Kristina. "If so, I can look into that. Is it your work hours or work location? Or is it me, would you rather work for someone else? Has your life outside of work changed?"

Jaime's response to each question was "no."

"What is it then?" asked Kristina, baffled. "What has moved you to this decision?"

Jaime took a deep breath. She decided to be truthful, given her concerns for the organization and because Kristina had always been honest with her.

"I've wanted to have a conversation with you before about how constrained and undervalued I feel in the way this organization functions. I even came into your office a couple of times to talk about my concerns, but the timing never felt right. But now, I feel like I owe it to you to tell you what led me to this decision. I'm tired of the naysayers. I'm tired of being overly controlled. I'm tired of being second-guessed all the time," she said. "When I first joined, I understood there would be some restrictions to what I could do because it takes time to learn about how an organization works. But now, after all these years, I thought my track record would be worth something—that you'd see what I bring and am capable of. I thought you would allow me to make decisions and move things forward in areas where I have knowledge and expertise, where I know my efforts would benefit the organization, and where I'm pretty sure you and others would agree with me or, at least, see my actions as viable. I need to have the freedom to act on the things I know are in the organization's best interests."

"But you have that now," said Kristina.

"No, I don't. Whenever I have an idea or want to make a decision in an area where I have knowledge, expertise, and prior experience, I still need your permission to act on it. You always say, 'Let's think about that,' or 'Can you explain that further?' I have to justify every thought. And often, even after that, you still want me to check with others. It's just a waste of time, and it frustrates me and saps my energy. I need to find a place to work where I can fully apply my knowledge and be valued. And there are other people here who feel this way, too."

Kristina was silent for a moment, thinking. Then she spoke. "I don't want to lose you, or other people who are talented like you, nor does the organization. You're too valuable."

Jaime said. "Then there are going to have to be some big changes."

Organizations Need to Get Different[5]

Many organizations in the United States and around the globe are receiving wake-up calls from dissatisfied team members who want more from their jobs, the organizations where they work, and their managers. You may be experiencing this in your organization. There are many people like Jaime who feel smothered in their jobs by unnecessary controls and microman-agement, and wind up feeling underutilized and un-dervalued. They are either speaking up about the need for change, or searching for jobs elsewhere—and organizations are paying the price. Many organizations need to transform the way they treat people if they want to keep talent.

Increasing numbers of people are redefining what work and job success mean. There is no disputing the fact that workforce conditions and expectations have changed dramatically in the last few years. Even before the 2020 pandemic, people had started to rethink their relationship to work, questioning the role it played in defining their identities, and re-evaluating how much energy they gave to work versus other aspects in their life such as family, community, self-care, and down-time. For many, the pandemic upended long-held ideas of where and how work could be accomplished, and with the introduction of remote work, virtual meet-ings, and hybrid workplaces, some of these aspirations have become realities, or at least possibilities.

Additionally, the discussion of inclusion has raised the bar on expectations in the workplace as organiza-tions have said they want employees to have a greater sense of belonging, a greater voice, and recognition for their contributions—and employees are holding them to that. Furthermore, people are looking for more independence in their jobs.

People Don't Want to Be Smothered

People want to be able to make choices and take actions they feel are right without a multitude of roadblocks or feeling smothered by their manager. Some people were given a high degree of latitude growing up, some were even allowed to become co-decision makers with their parents who gave them the ability to challenge and push back, and they expect that in the workplace, too. They have less patience to wait or ask for permission when they know they have the skills to do something. They have greater curiosity and ask questions—which some managers see as threatening or challenging. Many have grown up in a culture of customization, in which products and services are uniquely individualized, and so they expect that level of curation in their career paths too, along with greater focus on development and learning rather than tenure and rank.[6]

Technology and, more recently, generative artificial intelligence (GAI) have shepherded in a new level of speed and information availability that have contributed to higher expectations in accomplishing tasks, especially in individuals who have grown up with the internet and are used to things happening with speed. When people feel slowed down or thwarted in their ability to carry out their work effectively, they grow dissatisfied with their job and think about moving elsewhere.

Many people today view themselves as free agents in the workplace.[7] Just as in sports, in which players can move from team to team, so, too, do individuals see themselves as able to move between organizations quickly and easily, without the need to stay in one place. Many people are asking for a decrease in work hours and some countries are moving to a thirty-two-hour work week. Those who work on the front lines and in other positions that don't have the opportunity for hybrid work want to have a shorter work week, or some schedule that allows them to have greater flexibility in their lives.[8] There is a significant shift in what people need and want from their organizations to do their best work, and an incremental response will not do. The workplace must take a leap forward to address the needs of today's workforce.

Unfortunately, there is a disconnect between what people need and what many leaders believe is necessary or even possible. Leaders may see the need for change, but they also feel a responsibility to protect their organization and some of its practices. They may know that innovation is important for the longevity of their organization, but they feel they have to ensure it does not put the organization at risk, so they want everything checked and proven before it moves too far along. With this kind of thinking from their leaders, organizations risk operating too slowly as decisions are made only at the very top and innovations are not embraced. Capable and skilled people are often underutilized, devalued, and demoralized, leaving them with few options other than to contribute less, check out, or move on.

In this highly competitive and evolving world of work, it is no surprise that organizations are feeling extremely challenged, some for their very existence. To survive, they must continue to evolve, especially around manager-employee interactions. The old saying "people join organizations and leave managers" has never been truer. In today's work world, we consider all employees knowledge workers—individuals who use their expertise, critical thinking, and interpersonal skills to add value to their job. These capabilities are needed more than ever but, in many organizations, they are not valued as much as they need to be. As a result, when knowledge workers feel unheard, smothered, or aren't treated in a manner that *works for them*, they will make a move.

In recent years, we have seen knowledge workers struggling with how they are treated in many of the organizations where we consult. We believe unleashing the power of agency is key to reshaping our workplaces to meet the needs of individuals and teams, as well as the demands of a fast-paced, global economy. But what do we mean when we talk about agency? We define agency as:

Ensuring that all people, of all roles, levels, tenure, and identities have the power, influence, and voice to make choices and decisions related to their jobs and the betterment of their organization.

When everyone has agency, people know they are full and deserving members of the organization and their voice will be heard. With agency, every person feels a sense of ownership and accountability for the organization's success. They feel an obligation to share their thoughts and to make things better. They have the decision rights to make things happen within their area of responsibility, and improve things there and throughout the organization. Everyone's expertise is valued. They are the Operations Leaders of their jobs. Or as one of our clients defined it, people in the organization lead from any chair.

Chapter 2

Agency in Action . . . The Same Organization Five Years Later

Morgan is going into the office today as it is Collaboration Day. These monthly get togethers enable people to meet up in person and enhance connection, engagement, and trust. They are also an opportunity to introduce new employees, and help everyone get to know one another better, both professionally and personally, beyond the computer screen. Collaboration Days were established a few years earlier as part of the organization's transformation process to a culture of agency. Usually, there are team-building activities, including community service projects, as well as the opportunity for work teams to come together on projects.

Morgan is always excited to be at Collaboration Day as he looks forward to seeing people face to face. Most other days, Morgan works from home to enable the work-life-me integration he needs. He has spent a good deal of time in recent years reflecting on his life and knows now that he needs space for self-care and personal growth as well as professional development. Like many people, he has now added the "me" part to his equation of life which has enhanced his home and work life. Usually, Morgan sets his own work hours, which is helpful as he is an early morning person, often starting his day at 5:30 A.M. and then taking a break in the afternoon, but today he will be at the office for several hours beginning at 9:30 A.M.

Morgan enters the first meeting of the day, heading into the conference room where many of his colleagues are already gathered. As is the custom, everyone greets one another. Morgan says hello to Jaime, a newly promoted vice president who has been especially supportive of one of Morgan's recent initiatives. Since the last meeting, everyone has been working on their respective areas of responsibility and making the necessary decisions in which they have authority. Today, the team will share their insights and thoughts and inform everyone else about decisions made and actions taken so they can collectively identify the next decisions they need to make together. Morgan appreciates being part of this team and is excited to share what decisions he has made, and to hear and exchange ideas with colleagues. It is always stimulating to have everyone in the same room to do this and often these in-person meetings lead to new ideas, greater spontaneity, creativity, risk-taking, and problem-solving. There is energy and excitement when everyone is together; their team partnership deepens. These Collaboration Days are always worth it.

Fortunately, in addition to being open to flexible working hours and arrangements, the organization has a strong bias for enabling individuals and teams to make things happen. There are very few organizational hoops to jump through. People no longer need permission to send an email, or to speak to someone in another department, or to a senior leader. They no longer need multiple approvals from senior leaders to move a project forward, and people can make decisions at their level on most issues rather than having to wait for decision-making to bubble up through the organization.

The team meets for a couple of hours, talks through issues as they arise, brainstorm, and feels good about their work. As things draw to a close, Morgan thanks everyone for their input, then they all go off to other meetings or one of the special presentations given that day. Later, the team will reconvene for a collaboration activity as part of their paid worktime, a visit to a local shelter that provides meals for unhoused people. It is a further opportunity to engage with one another as a team and to enrich the community.

Morgan really appreciates working for the organization. He almost always has a sense of energy when going about his work. He feels more than listened to; Morgan feels joined, knowing his efforts are a vital part of something bigger. As he reflects on why the organization is so special these days, he thinks about having the ability to make things happen and especially values having the right to make decisions and the freedom to decide how to accomplish tasks. Morgan's manager, Stan, has done a great job of providing clarity on timelines and needed outcomes and lets Morgan determine how to meet and achieve them. Stan has worked hard to remove barriers that impede workflow and provides the resources and tools needed to work effectively and efficiently. Stan supports Morgan, joins him, listens well, and cheers him on toward higher performance, enabling Morgan to bring his thinking and creativity to projects. In response, Morgan has been able to do his best work, feels a sense of belonging with his team and the organization, and has a strong sense of autonomy, authority, and leadership in his role.

Morgan Values His Team Members

Morgan's team members are not only great colleagues, but they are good work friends, too. They are curious about one another's work and lives, cheer each other on, and do everything they can to assist each other in doing their best work. There is a level of trust and partnership present that enables each person to act with autonomy within their areas of responsibility and expertise. Each person takes ownership of their job and likes having accountability. In turn, this encourages them, individually and collectively, to take more risks. People feel the freedom to think creatively, and, if they make mistakes, they are encouraged to use those as a learning opportunity. The colleagues give one another the benefit of the doubt, believing that each team member has something to offer. They work from the new organizational values of employing curiosity and respecting one another, rather than challenging or criticizing new ideas from the outset.

The Organization's Transition to Agency

The organization has deliberately enabled agency throughout the workplace. This was not always the case. Just a few years ago, things were very different. Facing an exodus of people who felt frustrated at not being able to do their job because they felt smothered and constrained, along with lackluster organization performance, senior leaders realized the organization itself was at risk. Something had to change. The organization began a major effort to transform how people interacted and worked together, one that moved away from how things had been done historically. This led to Stan and other managers significantly changing their leadership style, reducing their managerial oversight, and unleashing agency throughout the organization. This new culture now enables Stan to spend time coaching and developing people, connecting, and managing information flow so that decisions he and his team make have the biggest impact on organization betterment. Stan ensures that the right people at the right level get the information they need. In turn, this culture of agency enables Morgan and people throughout the organization to use their skills, knowledge, and expertise, while feeling valued and bringing value to the organization. It's a win-win situation.

Chapter 3
What Is Agency?

In the last chapter, we showed how agency can transform an organization and bring out the best in every member of the workforce. As the evolution of the organization and the manager-employee relationship continues, the concept of agency needs to be at its center. When people are not allowed to exercise their agency, they often feel smothered and retreat into the role of "doer," someone who completes tasks as told and raises any decision or action up the chain of command for approval. Their manager acts as a checker overseeing every decision, large and small, which ties managers up with unnecessary work. Meanwhile, the individual feels as if they are not the leader of any of their job responsibilities, which limits their voice and influence. In such an environment, people feel they need permission to take even straightforward actions. Lack of agency becomes the fence they need to continually jump, wasting their time and their manager's and, most importantly, leaving them feeling demotivated.

There have been attempts to increase the autonomy and authority of people—to empower them to do their jobs with little supervision—but in many cases organizations have overlaid continued control that limits and often smothers people's ability to take the reins of their job. People often feel micromanaged, while information they need is gate-kept until it becomes impossible or onerous to take the slightest independent action or decision. In the end, people become more risk averse, feel untrusted, grow increasingly unsatisfied with their job, and act in smaller and smaller ways. It is also expensive and time consuming for managers to micromanage. All of this impedes individual and organizational growth. This may seem like a familiar scenario for you or someone you know.

No Longer Hands and Feet

Much has been written about—and most people ac-knowledge the importance of—talent in organizations, and yet we often behave toward people in the same way as workers were treated at the height of the Indus-trial Revolution, as if they were only "hands and feet" expected to follow instructions and operate within a narrow bandwidth, with their actions reviewed and checked. While this process of oversight and correc-tion might have been necessary at the beginning of the Industrial Revolution, when many manufacturing processes were new and almost everyone was learning novel ways of performing their labor, as workers en-hanced their skills and many became knowledge workers, the appropriate shift in oversight did not oc-cur. Many managers continued to oversee people in heavy-handed ways that limited a person's capacity to learn and grow, keeping them boxed in roles that stunted their motivation, creativity, and imagination.

We still see this approach in many organizations today. We worked with a manufacturing facility where the lowest tenured employees had been there for more than twenty years. They had decades of work experi-ence, knowledge, and expertise at their fingertips and knew the industry and the organization inside-out, yet they still had supervisors checking and approving their work. Many of today's managers were managed in the same way and so they continue the tradition when they rise to managerial positions themselves. Some haven't learned to trust that people will do a good job if given the space and freedom to do so, and others feel it is in the best interest of the organization to tightly con-trol everything. There are multiple reasons for this style of supervision, and in many cases, it is so common in organizations that the idea of questioning it, let alone changing it, is difficult to contemplate. But the need for change is here. For too long, many individuals have been underutilized in organizations and they are not interested in feeling this way anymore.

When People Are Smothered in Organizations

Before we discuss changing the culture, let's look at some of the ways in which we have seen organizations make people feel undervalued and small. These include:

▶ micromanagement

▶ constant checking of work

▶ withholding trust

▶ expecting an individual or team to constantly check in

▶ expecting an individual to ask for permission before proceeding

▶ quashing ideas

▶ not inviting people to meetings where they have important information to share

▶ interrupting someone's contributions in meetings

▶ withholding people's decision-making capacity

▶ keeping people's jobs narrow and inflexible

▶ insisting people do things one way (often their manager's way)

- ▶ not allowing someone to take risks that might be the wrong direction or fail

- ▶ withholding information people need to do their jobs or to understand the broader context for their work

- ▶ limiting or denying important professional development opportunities

The Impact of Being Smothered

When a person is confronted by such management on a daily basis, they begin to change the way they view their job, their role within an organization, their aspirations, and even themselves. They may begin to respond by:

- ▶ feeling like they are not trusted

- ▶ not assuming new responsibilities

- ▶ not contributing their thoughts and ideas

- ▶ becoming unable to make decisions

- ▶ losing their self-confidence

- ▶ assuming only the boss knows the answers

- ▶ not taking initiative

- ▶ becoming frightened of not getting it right

- ▶ believing that their input is not valued and not speaking up when there is a problem

- ▶ being reactive

- holding back ways to make things better
- feeling disempowered and demonstrating low engagement
- finding excuses to do the minimum
- looking for jobs elsewhere that will value them

As you have likely experienced, when people feel undervalued, there are many negative repercussions for the individual and, ultimately, for the organization. Creating a work environment where people can do their best work and add their value is critical to an organization's performance at every level—from individuals, pairs, and teams, to the whole. People want to have the agency to fulfill the role for which they were hired. To be the Operations Leader for their job. Our aim throughout this book is to help organizations transform to a culture of greater agency, enable each person to unleash their own agency, and if you are a manager or leader, to create a culture which operates on people exercising their agency.

Agency in Action

It is crucial for everyone, no matter their level, to understand what agency looks like in action, what it brings to each role, and how it can revolutionize work performance by increasing job satisfaction, motivation, and commitment to an organization. With agency, people:

- feel trusted
- have autonomy and the permission to act
- feel responsibility for their output

- experience ownership of their job
- are trusted to come up with their own solutions
- have the authority and power to address issues and opportunities in their areas of responsibility and make decisions accordingly
- have choice in how they accomplish their tasks and work

When someone is able to exercise their agency, they know that they are a full and deserving member of the organization and their voice will be heard. They feel an obligation to speak up and raise tough issues when something is misaligned with the mission, vision, key strategies, and values of the organization. They feel a sense of accountability for their organization's success. They have the decision rights to make things happen within their own role, and to improve things within their area of responsibility *and* throughout the organization. When people can exercise agency, they not only can exhibit that for themselves but can influence and engage others in a way that unleashes agency for them, too. By unleashing individual agency, each member of the workforce can achieve their potential and the organization can grow in tandem with their flourishing.

What Does Agency Look Like?

You may have recognized yourself or some of your behaviors, or maybe your organization's culture, while reading our description of the effects of a lack of agency in the workplace. This is not unusual. Agency is impeded, in part or completely, in the majority of organizations. For the most part, managers, leaders, and organizations do not block agency intentionally. They are often carrying out behaviors or following managerial styles that have been reinforced by our work cultures over time, or are simply replicating how they were managed themselves as they moved through the ranks. If we are going to have organizations in which agency is the norm, it is important for all of us working in them to understand more about agency, what it is and is not, how to recognize it, how to unleash it within ourselves and others, and how to know when we are impeding it so that we can change our ways.

First, let us address the concern that many people have, especially leaders and managers, that chaos will ensue if agency is unleashed in their organization. It won't. Agency doesn't mean "do whatever you want." Nor is it about people using agency only for themselves and their own agendas. Rather, it is about people being instrumental in sharing the knowledge and skills that they possess and acting for the betterment of people and the organization as a whole. Enabling agency relies on unleashing each person's learning and knowledge, understanding the possible outcomes, and then deciding about what/how/if to act within parameters, and always aligning with the organization's mission, vision, and strategic direction.

Table 3.1 elaborates on what agency is and is not, and provides an overview of some of the key elements.

Table 3.1 Agency Is and Is Not

Agency Is . . .	Agency Is Not . . .
Having the latitude to do your job without asking for permission every step of the way.	Making decisions without parameters.
Taking ownership of your work. Being accountable for the actions you take, for successes and failures, and embracing opportunities to learn.	Taking action or making decisions without accountability.
Collaborating and informing others.	Doing it alone and not communicating with others.
Using mistakes or failure in a project as a learning experience.	Punishing people for mistakes or failures.
Having the freedom to think and innovate.	Being a doer with little or no latitude to improve things.
Colleagues sharing the right information needed for people to do their best work.	Colleagues using information as power, information, or status.
A kind organization—providing honest feedback and a willingness to address issues when a mistake or misalignment occurs.	A nice organization—protecting people's feelings or choosing comfort at the expense of being honest or raising concerns when they arise.
Knowing how your work is connected to the organization's mission, vision, and values, and how it contributes to the higher performance of the organization.	Seeing your work disconnected from a larger process.

(continued)

Table 3.1 (*continued*)

Agency Is . . .	Agency Is Not . . .
Making decisions with support and knowing others have your back.	Making decisions without the support of others.
Experiencing enthusiasm, curiosity, and desire for ongoing learning and professional growth.	Stagnation and lack of growth.
Being trusted to do your job.	People given little latitude and experience; overbearing oversight by managers.

Empowerment and Agency—How They Differ

Over the years, many organizations have talked about empowerment and have implemented it in different ways in the workplace, with varying degrees of success. Many of these empowerment efforts focus on managers *giving* people empowerment, i.e., "empower your people." Some describe empowerment as critical for marginalized or disempowered groups to *allow them* to have a voice and influence in various aspects of their work. In addition, empowerment efforts are often designed to increase an individual or group's self-esteem and self-confidence.

In one organization, Shauna was doing a good job, and the leader of her division noticed her contributions and gave her a greater leadership role on a project, telling her to run with it. While this was not the norm at her organization, her manager saw Shauna's potential and wanted to make sure she felt empowered to lead more and to know that the organization supported her. Unfortunately, most of her colleagues did not experience the same level of empowerment, trust, or support from their managers. In many ways, her experience was a one-off. In another instance of empowering people, a manager provided a platform for open collaboration and decision-making in which individuals were encouraged to contribute ideas that the manager would then vet. This increased people's self-confidence and motivation to successfully accomplish work tasks, but the manager made sure he still had control regarding what ultimately got acted upon.

As these examples illustrate, empowerment is frequently bestowed on individuals by others, and often by those at higher managerial levels. In contrast, agency is about unleashing individuals at every level to make decisions and to have influence and power. The real differentiator between empowerment and agency is that agency is unleashed and not bestowed.

While empowerment is clearly an important element for individual success, agency moves individuals and organizations to another level of interaction and performance. We see empowerment and agency differing in some significant ways in Table 3.2.

Agency exists in all of us. From the earliest stages of life, people demonstrate many of the elements that are critical to agency—social interactions and connections, curiosity, having preferences, self-awareness, decision-making, planning, goal setting, and expertise in their lives. As people develop, we nurture an ability to act intentionally, make choices, and shape our experiences, all of which are key aspects of agency.

Agency is not something you give to a human being. Instead, it is something to be unleashed in people.

Table 3.2 How Empowerment Differs from Agency

Empowerment	Agency
Is bestowed.	Is inherent.
Managers *give* people empowerment.	Managers *unleash* agency in people by removing barriers and providing resources.
Managers *allow* people to act.	Managers *support* people's agency when they act.
People's self-esteem and self-confidence is increased by being given permission by others.	People take initiative and exercise decision-making and autonomy, which leads to feeling trusted and being able to fully contribute.

While we can contain, limit, deny, or suppress someone's agency, we believe people are born with agency, with the power to make choices that impact their environment and to invent, enhance, and create based on their skills, knowledge, and will. We believe that for organizations to move to a higher level of performance, everyone within them needs to utilize their agency for the betterment of the organization and for their own personal fulfillment.

Although people are born with agency, they are often limited in their ability to use it. As children, parents or caregivers may have stopped them from exercising their choice to wear open-toed shoes on a snowy day, or at school they may have been constrained in their desire to sing while working on algebra, even though it helped them think. Agency is thwarted in many ways in many situations, sometimes for safety reasons or for the sake of the common good, and indeed boundaries regarding agency are needed. The workplace is no different. Organizations need to ensure people have a safe and productive work environment. However, when we begin to consider agency in the workplace, we can see that organizations limit agency so much that they are nowhere near any boundaries, let alone in danger of crossing them. Moving toward greater agency requires that everyone—managers, team members, and individuals—understand what agency means, how it can help in their own work and that of others, and to what extent it is fostered—or isn't—in our own organizations. From this foundation, we can begin to implement ways for people at all levels to exercise their agency.

Inclusion as a Foundation for Agency

In recent years, many organizations have focused on creating more inclusive workplaces. As we consider the role of agency in the workplace, it is helpful to understand the interplay between inclusion, diversity, and agency, and how they support one another. It is especially important to underscore here that you cannot have agency without inclusion[9] and the interaction safety[10] that enables people to speak up, share ideas and opinions, and take ownership of their work. We believe that embracing a range of human differences within the workplace and incorporating a culture of inclusion are the necessary foundations for shaping the high-performing organizations needed for today. To achieve that, agency is the next essential step. Let's break this down further:

There is a common example used to distinguish diversity from inclusion when illustrating how life needs to be different in organizations:

> *Diversity means that you are invited to the party,*
> *whereas*
> *Inclusion means that you are invited to dance.*[11]

A culture that supports inclusion provides individuals of all backgrounds with a sense of belonging and the supportive energy from others to do their best work. An inclusive culture seeks out different perspectives and taps into the skills of all members of the organization, leading to enhanced decision-making. Together, diversity and inclusion have moved organizations far in better utilizing human talent and potential. However, their benefits are hindered if people don't have the ability to bring and apply all their know-how to every situation. This is where we build on the work of diversity and inclusion by adding agency. If we continue with the metaphor of the party, then:

> *Agency means co-creating the party itself, having the free-*
> *dom to contribute wisdom based on knowledge and*

experience, and the authority to act, i.e., deciding on the venue, guests, food, drinks, playlist, and when to end the dance.

Agency moves inclusion one step further with a focus on both the independence of the individual and the need for interdependence with others to accomplish goals. With agency comes ownership and responsibility. People no longer feel like a guest at the party or the organization, or feel like the help, laboring away at someone else's direction. At work, agency creates an environment in which individuals have influence, can make decisions, and take the actions needed to do their job; in which they are the Operations Leader of their job, have the power to co-create with others, and feel able to act in ways that uphold the organization's values and further its mission, vision, and strategies.

It is true that there have always been some people who were able to bring their differences to work and experience inclusion—for example, individuals who might differ from their colleagues due to a different style, nationality, ethnicity, or educational background but who share a commonality of race, gender, and/or sexual orientation and therefore are accepted. However, most of the time, that inclusion, and leveraging and valuing of differences, has not been evenly distributed to individuals outside of that narrow bandwidth. The same is true for agency. Historically, agency has been unleashed (consciously or unconsciously) for people primarily on a hierarchical and/or a limited individual basis with the criteria of familiarity and personal trust playing a role. Usually, agency and work freedom have not extended beyond a limited circle. As organizations work toward a culture of agency, it is important to assess and acknowledge these biases and tendencies so that they can be addressed, and agency can be exercised by all.

When agency is a way of life, an organization and its people can excel. SEMCO, a manufacturing company in Brazil, began such an effort in the 1980s, delegating decision-making to employees, and is still thriving today. "Over the past decade, the company's sales increased by 600 percent and profitability by 500 percent. Equally impressive, with a current backlog of more than 2,000 job applications, SEMCO has had less than 1 percent turnover among its 3,000 employees in the last six years. Leaders inspire employees to assume ownership and responsibility. The company's CEO, Ricardo Semler, encourages employees 'to go with their guts' in their decision-making and where the focus is on performance and accountability." SEMCO demonstrates the application of agency and its long-term success.[12]

Agency is both a concept and a practice that will move teams and individuals forward in their contributions to, and impact on, the organization. For many organizations it will also strengthen their interactions and speed with customers, partners, other organizations, and the general public. As part of our consultancy work, when we ask leaders if their organization is inclusive, many will say "Yes!" and point to various programs and initiatives they have put in place to foster greater inclusion. These may include Employee Resource Groups, enhanced hiring and promotion processes, mentoring and coaching, and training and education. Inclusion is something that their organizations cannot function without in today's world. Yet, when we ask those same leaders whether agency is a part of their organization's culture, they indicate it doesn't occur to the degree that the organization needs. They acknowledge that agency is important for greater individual and organizational success at a time in which speed, higher performance, and workforce well-being are essential. They appreciate that, with agency, every person at every level is in the game, that there are no onlookers or bystanders, and that everyone can take leadership in their role. That agency brings out the full benefits of inclusion. They can see that agency is about making things happen, fully tapping into the wisdom of the people of the organization without struggling through bureaucracy. That agency enables people to have power and influence, no matter their role, to move ideas forward and take action. They can see the vital role that agency plays and that it is becoming ever more critical for success, yet they are far from having an organization in which it is the norm.

A senior executive leader who is working on creating agency within her organization commented:

> *Without greater agency, we cannot scale our business and grow. When we were a start-up, people had greater agency. As we are growing, I see the senior leaders exerting more control and assuming that people in the organization don't know as much as they do. If we don't create more agency, we will add less and less value for our customers and employees as we are stunted by a few people at the top. These few leaders can't innovate fast enough or keep up with the speed of change. If we had greater agency, I, as a leader, would not be making decisions about which I have little direct information or line of sight regarding their full impact. Now I spend a lot of time responding to emails, paperwork, and administrative duties. I don't have enough time in my day to respond to it all. With greater agency, we would have more pockets of innovation. We could work at a faster pace, and I could transfer what I know to others to build greater capacity. With agency comes two-way learning and a greater willingness to experiment and beta test new ideas. We would create an*

amplified learning culture. But we just don't seem able to unleash the agency we need.

This is not surprising. Engaging leaders to enable greater agency requires an enormous shift in organizational culture and managerial and leadership practices. It is a process that involves clarity of purpose, trust-building, clear communication, and a commitment to share power and decision-making. It requires having faith in people and getting out of their way so they can do their best work and make their best contribution to the organization's success. This isn't just true for managers, but for everyone in the organization.

A leader of one of our clients commented that, while they know agency is needed, they are far from making it a reality in their organization. In fact, they are not sure where or how to start the process. Another client said she feels the intention to move to agency at her organization is there, but they seem to be fumbling toward it. They understand the concept and how it would be beneficial for everyone and for the organization, but fostering and practicing agency is hard. What does it look like? How do they use it and when? What is the framework for unleashing greater agency? What are the parameters so that everyone is on the same page?

In the next section of the book, we provide a step-by-step organizational change process to move toward this new reality of having a workplace that you and others want to be part of so you can do your best work—a workplace where everyone can exercise their inherent agency.

Part II
Ten Steps to Unleash Agency in Organizations
An Overview

Unleashing the power of agency at every level requires significant culture change for most organizations. It requires people on the individual level to move to exercise their agency for themselves and in partnership with others, for managers and leaders to unleash agency organization-wide and for themselves, and for the organization to have the systems and processes that unleash, nourish, and support agency. It can seem so overwhelming that it is difficult to know where to begin, whether for individuals, teams, supervisors and managers, senior leaders, or the organization at large. In the next four chapters, we will move through each step in the process to unleash agency in organizations, outlining one element of change at a time and how to position your organization for the next step. We will provide examples of client stories throughout to walk you through the journey toward agency. Our aim is to support everyone in their quest to exercise agency, while acknowledging that the possibility of unleashing agency for everyone first needs senior leaders to commit to change, sponsor it, and provide a clear vision and roadmap so that an organization's culture can embrace greater agency. We discuss how to identify and understand the need for change within an organization and how to implement and monitor that change to provide continuous improvement along the way (Figure P2.1).

We begin the journey by having senior leaders look at where their organization is now, and seeing why and where they need to adopt a culture of agency before assessing what a culture shift could mean for their organization and its people (Step 1: identify the need for greater agency). This may include the need to educate senior leaders to understand how greater agency is a next step on the journey to higher performance and

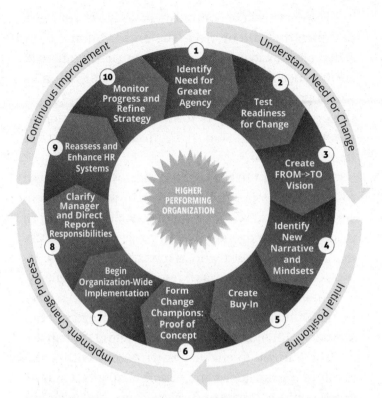

Figure P2.1 Ten Steps to Unleash Agency in Organizations

unleashing everyone's talents and abilities so they can do their best work.

Agency can't be bestowed or pushed onto the organization. It requires a dialogic process[13] that fully engages people in conversations as a critical component of change (Step 2: test the readiness for change; Step 3: create the FROM→TO culture vision).

The next critical steps envision an organization in which agency exists and is lived at every level, and communicates the payoff that it brings to both the organization and individuals (Step 4: identify the new narrative and mindsets to support the TO state; Step 5: create buy-in).

These steps take commitment to get them right, but once they are in place, the organization will be well on its way to understanding how agency can make a difference for everyone within the organization, at which point it will be time to roll it out across the entire organization (Step 6: form Change Champions—proof of concept; Step 7: begin organization-wide implementation).

At this point in the process, there will be the need to focus on people and management practices to ensure that the necessary support mechanisms are in place to enable agency in every role (Step 8: clarify manager and direct report responsibilities; Step 9: reassess and enhance human resources [HR] systems).

Finally, when everything is up and running, it is a matter of monitoring progress and adapting as necessary (Step 10: monitor progress and refine strategy).

The journey to enable greater agency will be difficult for organizations and people at all levels as it requires culture change. However, in organizations where we have seen aspects of it realized, it is well worth the time, effort, and commitment. Ensuring a culture of agency enables organizations and the people who work within them to achieve a new level of individual and team freedom, speed, and performance. It unleashes people's ability to do their best work. Everyone can give more to their work and their colleagues, and have the opportunity to share the wisdom they possess individually and collectively. When some of the current organizational restraints are removed, all people and the organization soar.

Chapter 4

Steps 1–3

Understanding the Need for Change

In this chapter, we introduce the first three steps of the agency in organizations process as the organization assesses its need for change and receives input and feedback.

Step 1: Identify the Need for Greater Agency

The first step on the journey to a culture of agency is for senior leaders to decide if they are willing to put in the effort to make the shift and embrace the organization culture that will come from unleashing agency in their organization.

> Change is happening: is the change leading you or do you want to give leadership to that change? I want to join the change and influence it.
>
> Rich Dewey,
> CEO of New York Independent System Operator, which runs New York's extensive and critical power grid

We have seen that considerable change is already underway in organizations, both in the speed at which work needs to be done, and in the needs and mindsets of people. The COVID pandemic sparked rapid change for some organizations and accelerated change for others. Some were already thinking about greater participation and inclusion of people in the flow and thinking of the workplace and the pandemic said, *speed that up*. The work contract between individuals and their employer was already under pressure to be more favorable to employees—once again the pandemic said, *go faster.* A renegotiation with the workforce is taking place. There is no longer an assumption that work only gets done if everyone is in the office five days a week. Now we see a hybrid work model and some countries moving to a four-day work week. There are so many variations on how, when, and where work gets accomplished, and organizations must respond to the new work patterns.

With the emergency stage of the pandemic over, some organizations are defaulting to the past or not being proactive enough about creating the culture that is needed now; but the reality is that organizational cultures are *already* changing. People have already shifted in their way of thinking regardless of whether organizations and leaders have shifted with them. Today's leaders have to position themselves and the people in their organizations to move through these changes in a timely and productive way. Sitting back or going too slowly means the changes—the culture and the current and future needs of the organization—will be moving out of sync leaving the organization at risk.

If we recognize that there will continue to be increased workloads due to the complexity of the nature of work and the speed of change, then organizations will need to find ways to invent and reallocate time as many of them are cautious about hiring more people. As a result, many people's roles have expanded to take on two or three jobs. Many people function today with to-do lists that go far beyond what any one person can accomplish, and they experience the accompanying burden of higher degrees of stress, overwork, and frustration. What if there were a way to address speed, reduce workloads, and attend to people's needs at the same time? One way to do so is to unleash agency so that people can more fully contribute their talents and skills and do their jobs in the best way possible.

As your organization begins to think about agency, the first question to ask is whether you have the right culture to support the changing needs of the work-force, one that enables people to do their best work in service of the mission, vision, and strategic direction of the organization. If not, what modifications need to be made in how people lead and manage to accomplish an organization-wide culture change?

Many organizations may be unaware of the barriers they have created that limit the exercise of agency.

Obstacles to Agency

▶ A lack of interaction safety may mean many decisions are pushed up the organization to managers and senior leaders because people fear making a wrong decision and being punished for it. They feel safer when others make the decisions because they can always say, "I was just doing what I was told."

▶ Bureaucratic "red tape" may exist that makes raising an issue not worth the effort.

▶ Those who have exercised agency in the past may have been burned, experiencing a metaphorical "slap on the wrist" (or more severe disciplinary action).

▶ Some may have been discouraged from exercising their agency, or have received either explicit or implicit messages to stay small in their roles, so they have given up and stopped trying.

- ► Some in the workforce may be skeptical that real agency is possible and will not believe it until they experience it—and most likely will need to experience it again and again.

Are senior leaders willing to address these and other barriers to make changes? Here are some ideas about how senior leaders can make this decision:

- ► Visit and talk with leaders in other organizations in your field, as well as in other industries, to learn about potential new ways of operating.

- ► Understand what other leaders are learning along the way as they implement agency.

- ► Assess whether your leadership group is willing to change by discussing what's been learned from external data-gathering, and what are the possible payoffs for the organization that would come with increased agency.

- ► Begin to understand the potential payoff for your organization that comes with undertaking a change effort toward greater agency, such as the ability to have a more efficient organization, make decisions faster, let people do their jobs more effectively and accomplish their best work, have more engaged people, and free up time so leaders can focus on critical opportunities that will enhance the organization.

Test
Readiness
for Change

Step 2: Test Organizational Readiness for Change

Some people in the organization might have been trying to exercise agency already. However, without organizational and senior leader support it's been a risky effort; in fact, some have already given up. Once the senior leaders have made the decision that change is necessary and they are willing to move forward, it is time to test the readiness of the organization by tapping the thinking of a subset of the organization—thinking partners.

Thinking partners are a diverse group of high-potential, high-performing individuals from various levels of the organization. Begin by identifying a group that is representative of the organization from various functions, backgrounds, and identities—around 30 people for most organizations; 12 for smaller organizations. Depending on the size of the organization and its geographical locations, it may be useful to engage several cohorts of such groups in various regions. Once they have been identified, interview them (individually, in subgroups, or as one large group) to learn about their experiences in carrying out their work.

Questions for Thinking Partners

These are examples of questions you might ask the thinking partners:

- ▶ What barriers do you experience in your ability to do your best work?

- ▶ What percentage of tasks do you have to ask for permission before executing?

- ▶ What information that you need to do your job is withheld from you, or only available if you go to great lengths to discover it?

- ▶ How does bureaucracy or the organizational culture hamper the working connections you need with various teams or individuals?

- ▶ When do you feel your expertise or experience is discounted or not heard?

- ▶ How would being able to exercise greater agency enhance your ability to carry out your job responsibilities? (Share the concept and definition of agency.)

After meeting with the group, reflect on the conversations with the thinking partners and what you have learned from the conversations about the level of autonomy, authority, decision-making, and leadership people are able to exercise. It is helpful to note that if high performers are experiencing barriers, it is safe to assume others in the organization may be experiencing barriers to an even larger degree. Decide whether to go forward to the next step of engaging the larger organization in the change process and creating a FROM→TO culture vision. If it seems that there are too many barriers, identify what barriers you can remove and work toward removing them. Note that these barriers are not only hindering the possibility of greater agency but most likely are hindering other areas of performance, and so they should be addressed.

Create
FROM->TO
Vision

3

Step 3: Conduct Organizational Dialogues to Create the FROM→TO Culture Vision

If senior leaders decide to move toward a culture of agency after hearing from thinking partners, the next step is to create a FROM→TO culture vision. In this way, senior leaders will have a clear idea of what they are trying to achieve for the organization and the necessary roadmap for getting there. The following processes are iterative and generative—information is shared back and forth with the purpose of enhancing the learning that is being gathered through the dialogue-group conversations (i.e., a catchball process).

To create a FROM→TO culture vision statement, the first step is to conduct an organization-wide dialogue through small group discussions to hear the voice of people in the organization. The aim is to learn more about the current state of the organization's work culture and to co-create a vision of what a culture of agency should look like as part of the new way of operating. Dialogue sessions would be conducted by either internal and/or outside facilitators and structured to include many people across the organization. Convene groups of eight to twelve people, ensuring there are no reporting relationships in any given group. Facilitators work to create interaction safety, so people feel free to speak up and share their thinking. Begin by discussing what people need to feel safe and provide assurances about confidentiality, i.e., comments will be reported anonymously and not attributed to individuals. Facilitators should invite people who prefer to share privately to contact them outside of the group.

Once groups are ready to commence discussion, provide an overview of the purpose for the change to greater agency and begin to engage the groups with some starter questions:

▶ What are you experiencing on a day-to-day basis that makes it easy to do your best work?

▶ What are the challenges to accomplishing your tasks? Why are they there? Are they adding value?

▶ If the challenges and/or barriers were not there, what would you and the organization gain?

▶ What would need to be different for you to have greater autonomy, authority, and leadership in your role?

▶ If you were able to exercise greater agency, what would you be able to accomplish that you can't do now?

▶ What two values or elements of the organization related to information sharing, decision-making, and accountability are important for the organization to maintain?

Upon completing the conversations, the senior leaders meet with the thinking partners and incorporate what they have learned from the organization-wide group dialogues into a draft FROM→TO culture

Table 4.1 FROM→TO Culture Vision

KEEP

Taking care of our customers.
Spirit, pride, determination, commitment, passion, and integrity.

CHANGE

FROM	TO
Leaders and managers micromanage.	People have responsibility and freedom over their areas of responsibility.
People have to ask permission, even within areas of expertise.	People act with autonomy when they have the expertise to do so.
People are punished for mistakes.	Mistakes seen as learning opportunities and trying new approaches is embraced.
Decisions are pushed up the organization.	Decisions are made at the right level; people have the autonomy to make decisions in their area of responsibility.
Leaders feel they must have all the answers.	Leaders are willing to say they don't know and seek and listen to the wisdom of the team.
Someone else's problem.	Each individual takes account-ability, responsibility, and owner-ship for their work and how their work connects to the whole.
Leaders don't give people the benefit of the doubt.	Leaders give the benefit of the doubt and extend trust.
Meeting conveners are not intentional about who is invited to meetings or about using others' time wisely. They invite more people than necessary as a way to be inclusive.	Conveners have the ability to differentiate the needs and skills of others to include the right people in a meeting.

vision that outlines the core elements of the new culture. When creating this FROM→TO chart, it is important to identify not only what needs to change to move to greater agency, but also what is of value from its current state that the organization wants to keep. Table 4.1 is an example of a FROM→TO culture vision.

Once the senior leaders and the thinking partners sense that the FROM→TO culture vision is directionally right, it is ready to be shared with the organization-at-large for their thoughts and feedback.

Chapter 5
Steps 4 and 5
Initial Positioning

In this chapter, we introduce the next three steps in the change process. We consider what the organization will need in order to move forward, create buy-in, and start to engage the larger organization.

Step 4: Identify the New Narrative and Mindsets to Support the TO State

Having outlined the FROM→TO culture vision, the next step in the process is for senior leaders to create a new narrative that inspires and engages the organization to move forward. Include the original thinking partners along with some additional members who stood out in the dialogue process to collaborate with in order to identify the new mindsets that will be needed to achieve and support each aspect of the TO state.

As part of the shift toward greater agency, there needs to be an understanding that new mindsets are necessary to support the new culture and the TO state. Everyone within the organization will need to change the way they do their jobs and *Get Different*, how they interact with others, and how they think about their individual and collective roles. There will be new definitions for what it means to be a manager, and a team member. A recent study indicated that there is an ongoing shift in a manager's role from being supervisory to collaborating and coordinating across units.[14] As organizations have flattened, a manager's span of control has increased. Managers now need to spend more time coaching and developing people, creating and fostering a culture of inclusion, and managing conflict and change. With these changes comes the need to recalibrate the managerial role and mindset. Likewise, there are shifts in the roles of each person, including a greater emphasis on collaboration, the development of an environment of interaction safety, and the ability to hear and listen to all colleagues.

Often, when looking at the FROM state, people see the various ways in which the current reality undermines their ability—and that of others—to fully contribute to the organization's performance. It can be an eye-opening experience. Through the dialogue session regarding how to create the TO state, it becomes clear that mindsets need to change at all levels of an organization in order to achieve that TO state.

As the thinking partners and leaders identify new mindsets, they need to bear in mind that several of the current mindsets need to transform to:

- ▶ sharing information with others as a key component of accomplishing one's tasks

- ▶ viewing people as trustworthy, as willing to do their best and take leadership in their role

- ▶ supporting a culture of interaction safety in which people feel safe enough to speak up, raise issues, and engage in conflicts and disagreements when they occur

- ▶ emphasizing that with agency comes greater responsibility and an obligation not only to do one's job well, but to partner and collaborate with others

In the beginning, some individuals might be skeptical about the changes or feel reluctant to implement them. However, as they start to see and experience change, they too are more willing to support the culture change. All leaders and managers will need to demonstrate a shift in mindset to unleash agency for others, and individuals will need to embrace their new agency and step into their jobs with more autonomy and responsibility.

Over time, as these new mindsets start to emerge, the organization needs to make them visible by connecting them to how they support the TO state. For example, when people embrace new mindsets of having autonomy, authority, and leadership in their roles, what flows from them are new behaviors of inclusion, trust, seeking out other voices, and sharing information and collaboration. They recognize the accountability that comes with their role and start to fully engage by initiating actions, communicating and partnering with others in the organization to achieve objectives, and investing more of themselves in their daily work.

One leader we work with talks about how this sense of agency shows up in a meeting:

> If I invite you to a meeting, you have a seat at the table.
>
> If you have a seat at the table, you need to bring your voice.
>
> If you bring your voice, I need you to bring your thinking.
>
> That is why I invited you to the meeting.
>
> Tom Scheetz,
> Principal, Wapiti Ventures LLC

This is the change in mindset we are aiming for with a culture of agency—for everyone to be able to share their knowledge and expertise for the good of the organization; for leaders and managers to understand that everyone has expertise in their role and value to the organization; and for individuals at all levels to be able to fully invest themselves in their jobs. It may take some time for people who aren't used to being asked to speak up, or to being heard, to feel comfortable in the new culture, but that is part of the change. Inviting everyone to speak at a meeting supports hearing everyone's voice. Having this expectation of interaction aligns with working toward the vision of unleashing everyone's agency.

Create a New Organizational Narrative

Using the input of the dialogic process, the FROM→TO culture vision, and new mindsets and behaviors, the next action is to create a draft organizational narrative (Figure 5.1). This will clearly lay out the story of the journey toward agency and the role every person plays in achieving the FROM→TO culture vision and a higher-performing organization. The draft narrative draws from the organization's vision, purpose, and values, and what will be different in the new state. It serves to inspire people within the organization, to articulate the payoffs for them and the organization as a whole, and to drive new mindsets and behaviors. Most importantly, it is a written document that provides an aspirational and achievable future, and serves to engage the organization and all its members as they embark on the journey of change to greater agency.

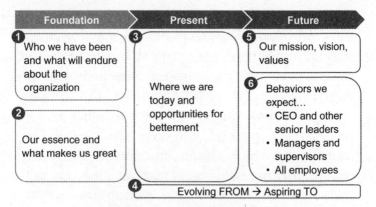

Figure 5.1. Elements of the
Organization Narrative

Once the new narrative has been created, it is essential that the senior leaders reaffirm their commitment to the proposed changes. They do so by convening the leadership group to reconfirm what they have learned so far in the process of engaging the dialogue groups, creating the FROM→TO culture vision, identifying the new mindsets, and ultimately—and most importantly—aligning on the new narrative and the payoff for the organization in undertaking the transformation to agency. Only after having recommitted to the change journey can they effectively engage the larger organization in the process, because once they raise expectations for everyone, they are at a point of no return. If they don't deliver, their credibility and trust will be significantly damaged, and recovery will be difficult.

For example, in one organization, as we talked about change, people often commented that the organization hadn't done well with big change initiatives. They explained that in several previous major change process undertakings, resistance to change had undermined progress and results were significantly less than anticipated. The leaders had said the right things, but their follow-through was lacking, and people had not taken the change seriously. When it came to initiating the agency-change process, it took considerably more effort and assurances from senior leaders to start things moving, and the dialogic engagement of everyone in the organization took concerted time and effort. This time, the senior leaders understood how important it was for them to be clear and steadfast about their commitment to the change and they were able to obtain successfully the needed buy-in.

Step 5: Share Results of the Organizational Dialogue to Create Buy-In and Engage the Larger Organization

Now is the moment to share the draft organizational narrative, the FROM→TO culture vision, and the new mindsets and behaviors to energize the organization and discuss what the future will hold.

This is a time for leaders to talk about their hopes and expectations for the new narrative, how they themselves will be different, and how the organization and individuals at all levels will need to get different and change.

> The mass of people always win in an organization.
> Hal Yoh,
> CEO, Day & Zimmermann

It is also a time to listen to questions and suggestions from people in the organization and consider whether any changes or additions need to be made to the narrative. Throughout this process, it is imperative that people have an opportunity to speak up and bring their innovative ideas to the conversation to assist in co-creating the new narrative. This highlights agency in action as people are able to exercise their own agency within the organization, some for the first time. Sharing the organization's change effort can be accomplished by:

- ▶ conducting town-hall meetings to roll out the new narrative, FROM→TO culture vision, what agency is and is not, the new mindsets for change, and what behaviors will be needed of each person in the process

- ▶ communicating the new narrative and direction via organizational newsletters, emails, and other channels (transparency is key, as are realistic expectations combined with enthusiasm for the direction the organization is heading)

- ▶ sharing the next step in the journey—forming Change Champions to test through a proof-of-concept experiment with a subset of the organization—and letting people know they will be kept apprised as the process goes forward

Chapter 6

Steps 6–8

Implementing the Change Process

It is time for the leaders to recommit to agency for all and how to best implement the change for your specific workplace. In this chapter, we begin to experiment and prove the case for agency. We share steps to bring the entirety of the organization on board and assist managers and individual contributors in understanding how they fit into the change process.

Step 6: Form Change Champions: Proof of Concept

After the initial buy-in from the people of the organization to the enhanced direction and the new narrative, the next step is the implementation of actions to move toward the new culture. While the organization is formally involved in the transformation process, there are individuals who already have been practicing agency. However, without the support of the organization and its systems, they are taking a great risk and often fail, or are isolated. At this stage, leaders need to be aware of how people in the organization, including themselves, may be affected as change starts to become real. Some people will be excited about it and think it's about time it's happened; others may be skeptical and adopt a wait-and-see attitude, not believing that change is possible; and still others may think the organization is fine as it is, feel comfortable with the status quo, know how to be successful in the current reality and, therefore, will be resistant to change. All these perspectives need to be addressed.

In the proof-of-concept stage, it is important to experiment with different ways in which the change can be implemented and to test for elements that can be strengthened or improved. Throughout this stage, attention needs to be paid to what is working well and what is not working as expected.

To begin the experimentation and implementation process, leaders need to identify an organizational unit—a "pocket of readiness"—that is willing to be a proof-of-concept experiment. Within that unit, a Change Champions cohort is formed to shepherd the change process and model the new behaviors, along with a senior leader to serve as an Executive Sponsor. Change Champions are internal-change role models who serve as catalysts for the change by participating in an education- and strategy-implementation process, and applying their learning to foster and practice agency in their day-to-day work.[15] The Executive Sponsor gives their perspective and provides support to the Change Champions cohort as they challenge the status quo, enabling the Change Champions to go about their work with backing from the upper levels of the unit. Together, the Change Champions and Executive Sponsor start a process of continuous learning and assessment of how best to implement the new narrative in the larger organization. The Change Champions cohort and Executive Sponsor also identify opportunities for change and how agency can enhance individual, team, and organization performance, and share those opportunities with senior leaders.

Change Champions are people who have influence with their peers, are willing to experiment with and model the necessary new behaviors and mindsets, and will advocate for the benefits of change through their actions and words. Over time, these individuals will be the trailblazers who are living the new narrative, providing examples of success that others in the larger organization can learn from and follow, and offering feedback on the practice of agency through teachable moments. It can be difficult at times to be a Change Champion—they can be viewed as rocking the boat or interrupting what feels familiar and comfortable. It is crucial that the Executive Sponsor provides visible support throughout the process and sanctions the Change Champions' actions as they go about their role and exercise agency. It is also important to ensure that the Change Champions' managers are on board with their role in the change process and encourage their increased agency in day-to-day interactions.

As part of the education, the Change Champions cohort creates a trusting and safe learning community where they can lean into change and support one another as they practice and advocate for greater agency throughout their unit of the organization. They model the new mindsets and behaviors with others in their teams and throughout the unit, creating buzz and energy. As people see and experience their colleagues' ability to be different and get results in an enhanced way, the support for and value of the change is accelerated. As others see and hear about these positive experiences, skepticism about change lessens and readiness to engage with the new ways of operating increases. They also create informal peer groups with whom they can share learning.

The CEO and the entire senior leadership team are obliged to be both major cheerleaders and sounding boards for the change process. Any inconsistent action on the part of the Executive Sponsor or senior leader may be seen as confirmation that it really isn't safe to change. From the outset, senior leaders have to be committed to showing support for the proof-of-concept units and the Change Champions cohorts as they behave in new ways. Both the senior leaders for the proof-of-concept unit, and for the overall organization, should model the new behaviors and mindsets themselves. Over time, this modeling creates trust and credibility with others in the larger organization, enabling them to be willing to lean in and try new behaviors.

The experiences of the proof-of-concept unit and the Change Champions begin to demonstrate how agency is making a difference in achieving individual and organizational goals and performance. The Change Champions start to make the new narrative more of a reality. Depending on the size of the organization, it may be helpful to do several proof-of-concept experiments in different units or geographies. For example, when working with a 29,000-person, multinational organization, we implemented regional proof-of-concept in different locations around the world to ensure that the new behaviors and ways of operating were aligned with the various local cultures. This allowed us to create multiple examples rather than trying a one-size-fits-all method which would have impeded attempts at change.

Step 7: Begin Organization-Wide Implementation

As the organization commits to the change effort, it is important to put change management[16] resources in place. These include making sure the change effort is sufficiently resourced, communication mechanisms are established, and a change management group is available. This group consists of individuals identified from across the organization to facilitate the implementation, support the continuous redesign of the change as needed, and monitor the change process.

Taking the lessons learned from the experiences of the Change Champion cohort, Executive Sponsors, and the pocket of readiness unit's application of agency, the organization makes any necessary tweaks, and then embarks on initiating the change process organization-wide.

To begin this step, an all-organization briefing is conducted to share the learning from the proof-of-concept implementation, explain what is next in the rollout of the culture of agency across the organization, and what is needed from each person to *get different*. An education process continues to create a common language and understanding about agency building on the previous step of creating buy-in (Step 5). This process needs to be multi-modal to effectively reach all organization members and provide them with a deeper understanding of agency—what it means, what it is and isn't, and the mindsets and behaviors expected of them. This might include webinars, virtual and in-person education sessions, reference materials, and self-directed learning, etc.

The next education initiative has organizational units create specific unit-level action plans. These plans focus on how to implement agency in every role, as well as what greater autonomy, authority, and leadership looks like for each individual and organizational unit. In these sessions attended by intact teams, people co-create how best to work together in this new environment and decide what they need from their team members and managers to be successful in their roles. Throughout this phase, as the effort to foster and exercise greater agency becomes the new way of operating, the CEO and senior leaders need to continue to encourage everyone in the organization to work together, even as things may prove challenging and unfamiliar.

Actions for Organization-Wide Implementation

Other actions at this stage are implemented by the change management group in partnership with the senior leaders, Human Resources, and internal communications as needed. These actions include the following:

▶ Communicating frequently via organizational newsletters, emails, and other channels about the new organizational narrative, learning from the proof-of-concept experiments, and the education- and action-planning process ahead, to keep people informed and engaged.

- Establishing a process for people to ask questions or raise concerns about the rollout or barriers they might be experiencing in moving toward the TO state, in addition to sharing success stories. This might include a message board where everyone can see and benefit from general questions and answers, and perhaps a separate chat line for more private/confidential questions.

- Posting information about the change effort in both in-person and virtual meeting rooms throughout the organization, including: the FROM→TO culture vision, the organization narrative, the definition of agency, and the necessary mindset shifts and new behaviors required.

- Creating pop-up messages on internal messaging systems about agency and stories of success.

- Creating a background screen that outlines elements of agency for people to use in virtual meetings.

- Designing and conducting organization-wide educational sessions for every person in the organization to learn about agency, with opportunities to practice the new behaviors needed for greater agency and ask questions. This should include virtual and in-person sessions.

- In addition to the general organization-wide education, developing specific education for managers that gives them the opportunity to learn what it means to be a manager in a culture of agency through case studies and role-play simulations.

Clarify
Manager and
Direct Report
Responsibilities

8

Step 8: Clarify Manager and Direct Report Responsibilities

At this stage, it is important to move to the individual level to ensure every person is clear on their role and has the necessary support to carry out their work responsibilities with agency.

Individuals and their managers or supervisors will look at each person's role and discuss how best to implement agency (see Chapter 8). For some people, it may be straightforward to fully exercise their agency, whereas there may be a learning curve for others. In each case, managers and team members will work together to identify learning milestones, support resources, and timelines needed to fully exercise their agency.

Similarly, teams will have conversations with their manager and with their team members about how they will independently and collectively exercise agency (see Chapter 9). They will identify how to work together to achieve shared and individual goals.

As part of this process, people need to set a schedule to check in with managers to discuss how their role and responsibilities are working and where to adjust them as needed. These check-in conversations are held monthly for the first six months and, subsequently, as people learn, and agency becomes more familiar, quarterly check-ins should be adequate—though everyone should be flexible.

Agency Coaches

Initially, as individuals, managers, and teams make the change to agency, it is helpful to develop a cadre of individuals who serve as "agency coaches" to provide support. This is a part-time role, implemented either by volunteers or HR staff. Agency coaches assist in the role-clarification discussion process as needed. They collect examples of how people are demonstrating agency. They also serve as a resource for people who are unsure how to implement new behaviors to exercise agency, as well as for managers who may need assistance in unleashing agency in their teams.

Leadership Feedback

Another method for developing greater agency and monitoring progress is by creating "leadership feedback pods." Each pod is a group of trusted peers, reports, and others that a leader brings together to receive feedback on their adoption and implementation of agency.[17]

To create a pod, leaders select a group of six to eight people from within the organization who reflect a diversity of functions, levels, and backgrounds and who all interact with the leader and can provide feedback based on their interactions. A leader's pod might include a peer in another division or department, a Human Resources team member, a direct report, someone who supports the leader from another function, and individuals at other levels of the leader's organization. It is important that the pod does not comprise the leader's direct reports. All pod members agree to be willing to provide feedback about the leader's behavior, both in areas in which the leader is doing well and where improvement or development is needed, so that the leader can continue to strive toward their learning and leadership goals, and consistently model and live the new behaviors and mindsets for agency.

Pods meet for an hour each month in the first year and then continue as needed. Many such leadership pods can exist within an organization, depending on the number of leaders who want to have this development opportunity. During these group meetings, the leader shares behaviors they are working on (e.g., not micromanaging; building greater trust; supporting others' decision-making) and receives feedback from pod members on where they are excelling, how they could improve, and discuss specific different approaches they could take. In this way, the leadership feedback pod differs from a traditional 360 in that it involves ongoing interaction from a trusted group of people who focus on the leader's current behaviors and provide real-time feedback rather than aggregated data. The spirit in which the leader enters this process is a key element in how successful it will be and in how authentic the pod feedback will be. Leadership pods enable leaders to adopt new behaviors more rapidly and demonstrate their willingness to be vulnerable, learn, and change. For many leaders, the level of honest feedback provided by the pod is something they rarely receive. In addition, the feedback pod benefits not just the leader but also the pod member participants who are stepping up to have honest conversations with the leader about the leader's behavior and their experience of how the leader is learning and growing. This reverberates not only in the pod but throughout the organization.

The process of moving to greater agency needs to be seen as part of an experiment in which everyone is learning how to move to the new culture vision. During this time of transition, people need to be given the benefit of the doubt as they experiment with a new way of interacting and taking ownership. Everyone should be encouraged to give themselves grace and expect setbacks and missteps as they navigate new ways of working and interacting. Whatever mistakes and missteps occur need to be seen as learning opportunities, consistent with the tenets and aspirations of a culture of agency.

Chapter 7
Steps 9 and 10
Continuous Improvement

As the organization has joined the change to utilizing agency, it now ensures the policies and practices within the organization support that change. As the new culture begins to take hold, it is time to look for ways to continually improve.

Step 9: Reassess and Enhance Human Resources Systems

While Step 8 occurs throughout the organization, Human Resources (HR) is focused on Step 9, where it assesses HR policies and practices, and makes decisions on what needs to change to move to the new narrative. More specific information about these changes can be found in Chapter 12, where we elaborate on HR systems and management practices. Below, we identify a few of the key areas that need to be addressed.

Hiring Criteria

The organization needs to hire people who have a desire to exercise agency (including taking initiative), are able to work both independently and collaboratively, and have demonstrated conflict-management skills.

Job Descriptions

Job descriptions need to reflect the demonstration of agency as a component of each person's job responsibilities. The descriptions will include the types of decisions that can be made by that role, as well as the decisions that must be made elsewhere or discussed with others.

Onboarding

As new people join the organization, content related to why agency is an important part of how the organization operates, and the expectations for each person to exercise agency, needs to be underscored and discussed as part of the onboarding and integration process. Managers in their interactions with new hires should also reinforce the importance of agency, as well as their role in removing barriers to support the individual in their ability to exercise agency.

Performance Management

Just as the elements of agency are a part of job descriptions, they need to be incorporated into the performance-management process, too, both in terms of goal setting and in the demonstration of agency in the accomplishment of those goals both individually, and in working and collaborating with others.

Promotion Criteria

The criteria for promotions need to reflect the new narrative and expectations. A major component of promotion criteria will become the extent to which individuals are exercising agency. Criteria for managers, supervisors, and leaders need to include the extent to which they are promoting and supporting a culture of agency with their team members and peers.

Success Stories

As the organization implements the change, people should share stories of success to highlight progress and show the ways the new culture is improving performance, decision-making, employee retention, and other key organization metrics.

Step 10: Monitor Progress and Refine Strategy

As the organization works toward a culture of agency, it is important to continue to monitor progress and refine the strategy as needed.

In addition to the individual check-ins outlined in Step 8, during which managers and direct reports clarify their responsibilities with respect to their roles and agency, we suggest conducting bi-monthly pulse surveys to assess how the organization is moving forward on the agency change process. The pulse surveys, and other such surveys, help to inform how the implementation is progressing and identify areas that might need to be refined to ensure the new narrative takes root. Many organizations use a third-party source to manage any potential for bias and ensure anonymity. These frequent surveys are administered to a subset of the organization on a rolling basis to identify opportunities for continuous improvement. Using a 0–10 scale (with 0 being low and 10 being high) people respond to statements such as these:

▶ Everyone in the organization is aware of what agency means.

▶ New mindsets and behaviors related to agency are becoming common practice.

▶ I see examples of how agency is leading to higher performance.

▶ I see examples of how agency is leading to increased motivation.

▶ My team members and other key partners exercise their agency.

▶ My manager supports me in my ability to exercise agency.

Statements about agency should be included in annual organization-wide surveys. Such statements might focus on tracking progress in reaching the TO state and identifying items that need greater focus and attention in the change process. Measured on the same 0–10 scale, statements may include the following:

▶ I am able to exercise agency as part of my job responsibilities.

▶ I have the autonomy necessary in my role.

▶ I am able to make independent decisions.

▶ I am clear which decisions I can make, which I need to collaborate with others to make, or bring to someone else to make.

- My manager supports me in exercising my agency.
- My colleagues exercise their agency.
- The organization culture supports me in exercising my agency.
- Decisions are made at the level where the best information is available.

Key Performance Indicators

It is also helpful to ensure that key performance indicators (KPIs) are in place to track and assess the impact of greater agency on the bottom-line measures that matter to the organization such as: error rate, time to market, customer satisfaction, innovation, safety, etc. Additionally, the organization will continue to support the change management resources to assess and monitor progress, and refine the strategy as needed.

Other Ways to Track Progress

Agency coaches need to be utilized to assist in problem solving and to make any barriers to agency clear to senior leaders, HR, and other key partners so they can be addressed. Conducting periodic listening sessions can assist in learning how agency is making a difference in the organization. Tracking the level of voluntary and involuntary turnover and retention rates, and inquiring during exit interviews the degree to which people were able to exercise agency and whether that was a factor in a decision to leave the organization, will help further the knowledge of how the culture of agency is taking hold.

The Commitment Curve to Mastery: Assessing Progress toward Agency

The Commitment Curve to Mastery is an excellent tool to monitor the progress of culture change (Figure 7.1). It charts people's behaviors along the path to new practices and ways of operating from awareness to understanding, experimentation, adoption, and to mastery and internalization. The different stages of the Commitment Curve (Awareness, Experimentation, and Mastery and Internalization) connect to the ten steps to unleash the power of agency.

Awareness

The initial Awareness phase includes contact conversations and people within an organization beginning to develop awareness that change is being considered or is in the initial phase of implementation. People are starting to understand the change and are developing a positive perception of the need for it to happen. This early phase relates to the following steps: Step 1: identify the need for change; Step 2: test for readiness for change; Step 3: create the initial FROM→TO culture vision; Step 4: identify the new mindsets and new narrative to support the TO state; and Step 5: create buy-in.

As these steps are implemented, people become aware of the need for change, what the change will mean for them, where the organization is trying to go, and the need for everyone to *Get Different*.

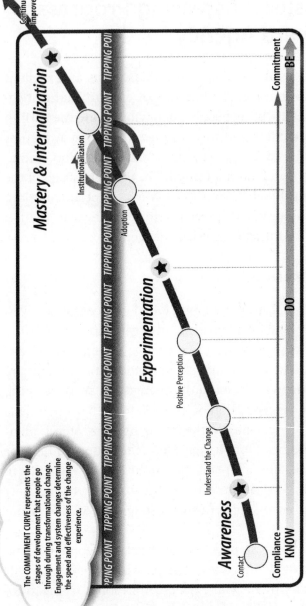

The COMMITMENT CURVE represents the stages of development that people go through during transformational change. Engagement and system changes determine the speed and effectiveness of the change experience.

Awareness

Experimentation

Mastery & Internalization

Continuous Improvement

Contact

Understand the Change

Positive Perception

Adoption

Institutionalization

Compliance

KNOW

DO

BE

Commitment

The STAGES OF DEVELOPMENT describe the behaviors that an individual, team/group, organization, and sponsor are exhibiting and how interactions are changing. There is a risk of people falling off the curve and losing commitment if engagement and systems are not sufficient.

Figure 7.1. Commitment Curve to Mastery

The Commitment Curve model is based on concepts from "Building Commitment to Organizational Change" by Daryl Conner, Conner Partners, © 2007–2011. Used with permission by authors.

Experimentation

Next, is the phase of Experimentation in which people practice the new behaviors needed for greater agency. They are starting to see what works and what needs to be changed to have greater autonomy, authority, and leadership in every role. This phase includes Step 6: form Change Champions: proof of concept and Step 7: begin organization-wide implementation. After the initial proof-of-concept stage, in which one or several units experiment with the change to agency, the change-implementation process expands to the larger organization so that more people experiment with the new mindsets and behaviors. At this stage, everyone is learning what greater agency means for them in their role and day-to-day interactions, and is having discussions with managers, team members, and others as they begin exercising agency.

Mastery and Internalization

The next phase in the change process is Mastery and Internalization, as the new way of being becomes second nature. This includes Step 8: clarify manager and direct report responsibilities; Step 9: reassess and enhance HR systems; and Step 10: monitor progress and refine strategy. For sustainable change to occur, the organization must embed the support and practices necessary for change in its systems and processes in order to institutionalize the new culture. As the new behaviors move to a level of mastery, the organization experiences the full benefits of the change effort. There is an ongoing focus on continuous improvement as the organization continues to enhance its overall competencies regarding agency.

By using this tool, an organization can assess where functions and units stand and can modify actions accordingly, ensuring people move along the curve and internalize the new behaviors needed to support and live agency. Data is useful to the organization at each phase of the change process. For example, if people fall off the commitment curve—through skepticism and/or resistance—leaders and the change-management team can assess what may be needed to bring them back, and how best to adjust the implementation strategy. They might ask: *Do they need more information to better understand the change? Are they having difficulty in experimenting with the new mindsets and behaviors? Are some functions moving further ahead and others lagging?* Diagnosing where individuals, teams, and functions are on the Commitment Curve enables a more tailored approach to adjusting the intervention and ensuring greater success. (Contact kjcg.com for more information regarding the Commitment Curve measurement tool.)

Together, these processes form the basis for continuous learning, identification of future needs, and refinement of the strategy. Measurement through the Commitment Curve, as well as pulse and organizational surveys, are all key parts of the change strategy and should not be skipped, no matter how successful the initial rollout seems to have been.

Part III
Cultivating Agency in Every Role

Now that we have discussed the need for agency in organizations today, defined what it is and is not, and identified the 10 steps to move organizations and their members to greater agency, we hope you are encouraged to move forward on individual, team, and organization-wide levels or that you have already started down the path to agency. In Part III, we turn to a discussion of the practical actions that individuals and teams, managers and supervisors, senior leaders, and the organization itself need to take to unleash agency.

One of our clients described having agency in the workplace as a gift—one that we all need to be able to unwrap and then be taught how to use. In Part III, we will support your journey toward change by focusing on bringing agency to each role within organizations—individuals, teams, managers and supervisors, and senior leaders—as each has different needs.

In the chapters that follow, we identify the constraints that may block agency in each role and the actions to take to make agency a way of life. In the resources section, you will find self-assessments to help you take a snapshot of where you are on your journey to greater agency and identify a strategy and action plan that moves you toward the outcomes that occur when agency is unleashed.

Chapter 8
Individuals Exercising Agency

In this chapter, we assist individuals at every level as they move to exercising agency in their roles within an organization. We highlight how agency can be impeded and outline the steps that can be taken to address such issues, as well as how to fully embrace autonomy, authority, and leadership.

When individuals exercise agency, the outcome is profound. When we have agency, we know we are trusted to apply our know-how and skills to our work. We can use our knowledge to innovate and solve problems. No matter our level within an organization, we are recognized for our contribution. With constraints and barriers removed, we are freed up to contribute more, collaborate more effectively, and add greater value.

Many of us come to organizations with a belief that we can add value by putting our skills to use, doing our jobs to the best of our ability, and providing great results. We are motivated to work and make a difference in an organization that supports us and sees our worth. We want to have control over the outcome of what we deliver and how we deliver it, and we want to continue to learn, grow, and expand our skills.

Unfortunately, as we have seen, many people feel underutilized and smothered. We often feel that we are not listened to, or we are interrupted in meetings— if we are invited to them in the first place. We are not fully respected for our expertise and experience, and we feel held back in our jobs, made to stay small in our roles. We often feel judged or blamed for decisions or ideas we might have and so we stop taking the risk to think at all. Some of us may feel we have been browbeaten and now are afraid to take even the simplest step toward greater responsibility and accountability for our work. This lack of agency can arise in several ways: in constraints put in place by an organization's culture; by a manager's mindset and behavior; and by our own thoughts, actions, and responses.

Unleashing Individuals' Autonomy, Authority, and Leadership

Table 8.1 provides some of the key constraints that get in the way of exercising agency for individuals as well as key outcomes that occur when people are able to exercise agency in their roles.

Table 8.2 shares some of the constraints that can impact an individual's ability to truly take ownership of their job, and the corresponding outcomes that can assist them in exercising greater agency.

Table 8.1 Organization Barriers and Benefits

Organizational Constraints to Achieving Agency	Organizational Outcomes with Agency
Work overload and accompanying stress.	Clarity of focus; right-sized workload.
Experience a blanket over them, e.g., need to get permission before moving forward; not permitted to take initiative; narrow scope of work; constant oversight from manager.	Able to work independently, with defined organizational parameters.
Experience being in a box.	Encouraged to bring thinking and innovation to every situation.
Punished for making mistakes.	Mistakes seen as learning opportunities.
Being second-guessed.	Trusted and encouraged to bring best thinking.
Pushing decisions up.	Making decisions at the appropriate levels.
Culture of fear.	Culture of interaction safety, with the freedom to speak up.
Not given the benefit of the doubt—being judged.	Giving the benefit of the doubt—being joined.
Conflict avoidance.	Addressing conflicts as they arise and working through them.
Holding on to the past.	Letting go of the past.

Table 8.2 Individual Barriers and Benefits

Individual Constraints	Individual Outcomes
Believing it's not your job.	Clear expectations of outcomes and boundaries.
Feeling that managers/ leaders won't let you do your job.	Acting and asking forgiveness if needed.
Feeling powerless.	Claiming your power, authority, and influence.
Not speaking up.	Every voice counts and is needed.
Avoiding responsibilities.	Stepping up to your role and responsibilities.
Staying in your comfort zone.	Willing to take risks and add value.
Staying small and not believing you have something to contribute.	Willing to grow and expand your capabilities—focusing on possibilities.
Mistakes are seen as failures.	Mistakes are seen as learning opportunities.
Focusing on limitations and barriers.	Focusing on where there are opportunities.
Fearful of being judged.	Feeling joined, accepted, and partnered with.

Nine Actions to Exercise Individual Agency

The steps below will help you as an individual take the reins in your work.

1. Do a self-assessment: When you feel you don't have enough agency, when you feel smothered, or you have a sense of frustration and dissatisfaction with your work, it is helpful to do a detailed self-assessment to find out exactly how and where you feel you are falling short. In this way, you can gain insight from data, and this will lead you toward finding solutions. In the resources section at the conclusion of the book, we provide a full assessment in Part A for individuals, but here you can begin by asking yourself these questions: How and to what extent are you currently exercising agency in your role? What is the level of autonomy, authority, and leadership you are taking? How much do you want to exercise?

2. Identify challenges and benefits: Identify the factors that affect your ability to exercise agency along with the challenges and benefits of exercising agency. Are you being prevented from exercising agency or are you being encouraged? How much of the problem is organizational? What are some of your concerns in exercising greater agency?

3. Talk with your manager: Discuss with your manager the areas you want to establish where you will use greater agency and brainstorm ideas for overcoming potential obstacles. Make sure you are

clear on how frequently you will check in and how best to ask for guidance when needed.

4. Understand boundaries: Identify with your manager the guardrails related to your area of responsibility.

5. Dialogue with your peers: Engage your peers about the agency you are each willing to exercise and how this might affect your collaboration and teamwork. What do you need from them to support utilizing your agency?

6. Communicate the "why": When appropriate, discuss your decisions and actions with others so they can more fully understand and, if needed, better connect their work to your decisions and yours to theirs.

7. Look for opportunities to share learning: Share knowledge with others so you contribute to enhancing agency for all. Are there ways you impact the ability of others to exercise agency?

8. Support others: Engage colleagues about what they need for agency and how you can support them.

9. Be honest about your learning curve: If you are struggling with some aspects of agency, say so. Be aware of how to get more support and mentoring. This is new and you are learning, so be gentle with yourself.

See assessment A in the resources section to assess the degree to which you as an individual are exercising agency.

Chapter 9
Teams Embrace Agency
We Are in This Together

Many of us work as individuals and as members of a team in our roles in organizations and, just as we need to unleash agency for ourselves, we need to do so for teams as well. It is important to acknowledge the delicate balance that comes with working and accomplishing tasks with others, the intricate dance of having both independence and interdependence. Not everything is a team task and sometimes we want to have the freedom to take our own initiative and actions when we are confident that it is the best course of action to get timely results; at other times, we will want to include others in our work. In this chapter, we look at ways to move teams to agency, at understanding individual and team decision making, how to resolve conflict around individual and group agency, and how to practice both autonomy and collaboration.

Table 9.1 looks at some of the key mindsets that can either constrain or enable a team's ability to exercise greater autonomy, authority, and leadership in its roles and interactions.

Table 9.1 Mindsets Needed to Unleash Team Agency in Organizations

Mindsets That Constrain Team Agency	Mindsets That Enable Team Agency
I can do it alone.	None of us is as smart as all of us combined.
The team will slow me down.	Complexity requires many different perspectives on the problem.

Table 9.1 (*continued*)

Mindsets That Constrain Team Agency	Mindsets That Enable Team Agency
Every voice does not need to be heard.	Let's hear from all the people who have information about the situation and can also add value. Right work, right people, right time, right tools.
It is okay not to share all the information that the team needs.	The more information shared, the better we, collectively, understand the problem and the better the solutions generated.
Everyone is not committed to the project.	Negotiate roles and commitment to the project, determining what is needed from each person and what they are willing to contribute. Establish each person's contribution to the whole—their piece of the puzzle.
People are overworked and don't have time for the team.	Clarify why each person is there, what they have to contribute, what is needed from them, and their time commitment. Negotiate time when possible.
We are not sure we can count on others to do their part.	Let go of people's past mistakes and/or address performance concerns.
The risk of failure is higher than if one person does it themselves.	The chance of success is increased when we fully include others with knowledge of the situation.
If one person does it themselves, they know it will be done right.	Each person only has one piece of the puzzle and there is no guarantee they can see the whole picture. Bringing the right people together to do the right work will exceed an individual's efforts alone.

Why Agency Matters to Teamwork: Unleashing Agency within Teams

Solving most organizational problems, exploring organization opportunities, and continuous improvement are almost always a team effort. As one of our clients said,

> The workplace needs to be a community of effort.
> Glenn Tilton,
> former CEO, United
> Airlines

By this, Tilton meant that the organization's mission, vision, and strategy are best accomplished by a group of people working together effectively. Although people may each hold individual pieces of the organizational puzzle, these parts only reach their maximum benefit when synergy is created—when people see themselves as part of a community of effort, of which the sum is greater than the parts. Underlying this statement is the understanding that the complexity of problems faced by organizations is too big for any one person to solve alone.

To perform tasks at a high level in a timely and accurate way, a team needs to have clarity of purpose and desired outcomes, as well as effective interpersonal connections and competencies. It is essential, therefore, that a team is clear about its agency from the outset so it can influence and advance the complex web of decisions, changes, and interactions most tasks require. Too often, progress is slowed by unnecessary meetings and reports with and for people who want to be informed, or feel the need to sign off on things, even though they are not a knowledgeable person about the issue or opportunity. Often this results in redundancy in the approval process. Before a project begins, get clear about where people have agency because it will provide the roadmap for how work gets done.

In many organizations, when a crisis or an urgent matter arises, the question of agency is seldom in doubt. In these instances, an *ad hoc* emergency team is formed and is given a clear direction, a timeline, and clarity about whom to report to. Often, the higher the level of leadership the team reports to, the easier it is to accomplish their task. That is because their agency is clear. However, that clarity does not always exist in day-to-day interactions. We have seen this scenario play out in many client organizations. One client, a utility company, was able to work together effectively across all the various functions of the organization in times of crisis, such as during major power outages. They each took leadership in their own areas of responsibility, made decisions on the spot, involved other functions as needed, and easily communicated across boundaries with other parts of the organization. Everyone was clear on their agency and their interdependencies. However, in normal times, the different functions did not work effectively together. They got in each other's way; people blamed one another and did not communicate concerns or needs to other areas. It was clear that the organization needed to have more clarity of purpose and address areas of individual agency, team agency, and overlap between departments for more effective day-to-day operations and interactions.

Twelve Actions to Exercise Team Agency

1. Build a community of trust, openness, and collaboration within teams as a foundation for success. This can occur through team-building activities and taking the time to discuss both group process and expected outcomes. It is important to get to know one another as work partners *and* as human beings.

2. Discuss with team members what agency means to each of them as individuals in accomplishing their goals.

3. Consider what agency means for the team in accomplishing their tasks.

4. Establish group norms for operating. Clarify how the team will work together, where it needs to collaborate, and how it will share information. Ask people their preferred style of interaction and working, and the strengths and qualities they bring to the team.

5. Review what each person needs to do their best work, including what they need to experience interaction safety and feel able to speak up.

6. Develop clarity about needed team outcomes. Clearly define tasks and develop a shared understanding of what each person's role will be in accomplishing these outcomes.

7. Identify individual and collective group agency, including how the team will make decisions, when individuals have the authority to make a decision,

and when something needs to be brought to the team for discussion and decision-making.

8. Create ways for how the team will address conflicts, misunderstandings, and disagreements that may arise related to individual and collective autonomy, authority, and leadership.

9. Decide on the frequency of interactions, preferred methods of communication (email, text, internal messaging systems, group chat, phone calls, virtual and in-person meetings, etc.) and when each method will be used (recognizing that not everyone needs to be included on everything).

10. Understand and clarify the role the manager (or managers) plays and how they need to be included. Identify additional key partners who need to be kept informed of progress along the way (including other functions, teams, and stakeholders).

11. Discuss how the team will monitor progress. Where does each member need more autonomy and independence? Where does each team member need greater collaboration and interdependence?

12. At the end of meetings, leave time to discuss how the meeting went, share appreciations to other people for their contributions, and be clear about next steps.

See assessment B in the resources section to assess how teams are able to exercise their agency.

Chapter 10

Managers and Supervisors

Cultivating Agency in Every Role

In this chapter, we focus on managers and supervisors and how to assist them as they cultivate agency for individuals and teams, *and* as they seek to exercise more agency in their own roles. It is important to acknowledge that managers and supervisors grapple with how to lead a workforce that is often less connected than previously due to remote/hybrid work, is more diverse, and has higher expectations of work satisfaction and employer support than ever before. Very often, managers find that old styles of managing are ineffective, and they must learn to embrace new ways.

The changing managerial role is key in establishing agency in organizations and it is essential that organizations take the time to define the requirements of, and challenges for, managers and supervisors as they work toward implementing agency. In a culture of agency, team leaders need to place more emphasis on their role of enabler, supporter, and developer of people. They have to connect dots across the organization and see how their team's work aligns with the organization's vision, mission, and strategy. They should seek to understand what motivates people and what each person needs in order to do their best work. At the same time, managers must focus on their own ability to exercise agency since managers, particularly middle managers, may struggle with juggling the dual demands of being accountable for delivering results through others and the pressures of responding to both their team members and their own manager's needs.

How to Cultivate Agency for Individuals and Teams

In one client organization, as a manager was working on supporting greater agency on her team, she quietly tracked all the decisions the team was asking her to weigh in on during a staff meeting. She responded to the queries, but at the end of the meeting she restated all the decisions they did not need her to make, underscoring that they had greater agency than they were exercising. It was eye-opening to her that her team felt the need to check in with her even when they had adequate experience and expertise to move forward independently. She saw that she hadn't sufficiently clarified her team members' roles and agency. She also realized it was going to take a lot more effort and time from her as a manager to help her team fully exercise their agency.

Even if managers want their teams and direct reports to have and exercise agency, it won't happen without intentional work from them as managers.

Eight Actions Managers Can Take to Unleash Agency with Direct Reports and Other Individuals

1. Once Human Resources has integrated agency into job descriptions and performance-management processes (see Chapter 12), discuss with direct reports what agency means for their role and objectives and how you will work to support them to exercise greater agency.

2. Clarify how your direct reports' work and objectives connect to the organization's vision, mission, and strategic direction, along with clear outcomes and timelines.

3. Ask people what they need to exercise their agency or to increase their level of agency—including what organizational barriers block their agency—and take steps to remove those barriers.

4. Create interaction safety so direct reports and others are willing and able to speak up and raise challenges, problems, and opportunities, and take necessary actions to move their work and the organization forward.

5. Identify and communicate the types of situations and decisions that need to be taken to a more senior level for discussion and for attention. In this way, the individual knows where they have autonomy to make a decision, and where others need to be included for broader gathering of information or for decision-making.

6. Openly discuss any concerns about moving to greater agency. Identify behaviors you personally want to watch out for as a manager—am I micromanaging? Am I providing enough coaching and support? Ask direct reports what they need from you as a manager, or from others, to enable them to step up to exercise greater autonomy, authority, and leadership in their role.

7. Identify areas where your direct reports would specifically like coaching and how you can support their development. Discuss what motivates them to do their best work and what they need for greater work-life-me integration.

8. Recognize that both you and your direct reports are experimenting with new behaviors and discuss possible barriers to and opportunities for exercising greater agency.

Mindset Shifts for Managers

Table 10.1 identifies the shifts in mindsets that are needed for managers and supervisors to create and support an environment in which individuals and teams exercise agency.

Often, managers have been in their roles for many years, and it will not be easy for them to change overnight. It can be helpful if they understand how their own behaviors limit agency generally and specifically so they might be more self-aware and catch themselves before they act. We have found that managers need to consider how they will change their behaviors in connection with:

► micromanaging

► feeling the need to have all the answers to every question

► acting as if people don't have answers

► communicating expectations

Assessment C provides a self-assessment checklist for managers and supervisors to use when considering

Table 10.1 Shifting Manager Mindsets and Behaviors

Current Mindsets and Behaviors	Needed Mindsets and Behaviors
Manager involvement in every decision.	Trusting people to make decisions.
Failing to address inconsistent and unclear boundaries and outcomes, and uncertainty about decision rights.	Clarity about boundaries, responsibilities, and desired outcomes.
Creating fear of speaking up.	Encouraging candid and open dialogue.
Dictating how tasks are done.	Providing clear expectations, timelines, and interim guidance as needed.
Lack of clarity about how an individual's work connects to the bigger picture.	Ensuring people know how their work connects to the organization's goals and objectives.
Reluctance to delegate.	Delegating with ease and enabling autonomy.
Expecting individuals to provide detailed information about every aspect of their work.	Hearing outcomes and headlines. Checking in as needed.
Untrusting of people's abilities and competence.	Believing in your people and supporting their autonomy and authority to act.
Avoiding mistakes at all costs, or punishing people for mistakes.	Seeing failure and mistakes as a learning opportunity.
Only accepting and supporting what has been done in the past.	Experimenting with new ideas and ways of working.
Maintaining power and control.	Partnering and collaborating.
Needing to know everything.	Trusting others' knowledge.

how they unleash and hinder agency, both in the organization and for themselves.

As managers are letting go of old ways of thinking and behaviors, they will need to enhance their skills in the following ways:

- ▶ Learning to cultivate trust.

- ▶ Slowing down to ensure others can include their thinking.

- ▶ Providing clear guidance on check-ins.

- ▶ Realizing there is more than one way to accomplish a task.

- ▶ Understanding that people are learning and growing, and they might make mistakes from which they can learn.

- ▶ Giving people the benefit of the doubt, and being curious when someone sees something differently.

- ▶ Learning how to be more appreciative and explicitly recognizing people's accomplishments along the journey to achieving results.

The impact of unleashing agency as a manager is profound. A client shared a story about one of their first experiences of being able to exercise agency and the life-changing way it affected their ability to do their job better. Their supervisor let them know she wouldn't be able to attend a meeting with various partners in the organization and asked them to go in her place. They had been to these meetings with her before as an observer. "You know exactly what to do," she told them, and she gave them a couple of bullet points she wanted them to share. At the meeting, when it was the client's turn to speak, they felt confident. The client knew their area of expertise, was well prepared, and had the support and trust of their manager. As they spoke, they felt they were listened to and seen as someone with knowledge and not just a stand-in for their manager. Later, as the meeting continued and someone else spoke, they felt confident enough to ask questions, get clarity on points, and discuss ways their function might collaborate in the future. They felt safe enough to speak and felt that they weren't in the meeting just as a representative but as a full member. This feeling of exercising their agency was exhilarating. Not only were they eager to exercise their own agency again, but they were now even more inspired to unleash agency in the team who reported to them.

The Importance of Trust

Many of the organizations we work with have cited "trust" as key when it comes to unleashing agency. When people feel trusted, a shift often occurs and there is a sense of belonging, of being valued. When managers and supervisors operate in an environment of agency, they trust their teams to make the necessary decisions at the correct levels. They don't feel the need to micromanage or to have individuals and teams check in or ask permission about every little thing. Individuals and teams are enabled to act decisively rather than delegate up out of fear of making mistakes. This allows everyone at every level to get their own work done, enhancing productivity, morale, and well-being.

One manager who has been working on unleashing agency with their direct reports has been focusing on increasing trust with their team. As they say, "Trust is a huge piece of creating agency." Recently, the manager decided to make some changes around spending limits. In the past, people had needed to ask their permission for every budget item. However, after conversations with their team members, they decided together they each had the authority to spend up to $500 annually on anything they felt they needed for their roles. The manager trusted they would use the money to do their jobs better and provide greater value for their customers, which they did, and their team members appreciated the manager's trust in them.

Connecting to the Organization's Vision, Mission, and Values

To increase agency, it is important for every person to see how their work connects to the organization, and managers and supervisors play a crucial role here. They need to help their direct reports and teams understand the impact of their roles in the bigger picture of the organization by focusing on three key areas:

- Identifying the mission, vision, values, and strategic direction and the way that each person's work connects to them.

- Connecting the organizational dots so everyone knows their key partners for performance success: who to talk with, learn from, and problem solve with given the problem or opportunity they are addressing. Ensure that barriers that prevent access are removed.

- Providing coaching, mentoring, and feedback to assist people to grow and develop in their jobs and beyond.

When the boundaries are well-defined, people can more easily exercise their agency and apply the skills and capabilities for which they were hired. They feel greater freedom and confidence to address the challenges and opportunities that exist today, as well as those that are gathering on the horizon.

When Things Don't Go Well

Unfortunately, unleashing agency does not always run smoothly, and managers may have to adjust accordingly. As an organization moves to agency, a manager may experience enthusiasm for change from some people but may discover resistance from others. Not everyone is looking to exercise agency in their role. Some people may seemingly just want to punch the clock and/or stay in their lane. In such situations, it is important for managers to be willing to engage, be open-minded, and listen for what might be holding people back from exercising greater agency. For some, their hesitancy may arise from previous negative experiences in which they tried to exercise agency and were reprimanded or disciplined for it; others may not be fully clear on how they can exercise agency in their role. In each instance, truly listening to someone's needs is key to engaging and partnering with that person. It may take some time, and managers need to be available for frequent check-ins and discussions, and provide access to further support and resources. In addition, managers should not take someone else's resistance to change personally or see it as a failure on their part.

Five Actions Managers Can Take to Unleash Agency with Team Members

In the previous chapter we identified some of the actions that teams can take to clarify how they will exercise agency as individuals and as a team. Below we discuss how managers can play a part in supporting teams to exercise greater agency.

1. Encourage teams to slow down and spend time connecting and learning more about one another, instead of jumping right into the task. As part of this process, the manager might share what they think each person brings to the team.

2. Lay the groundwork for the team by discussing with team members the boundaries, goals, and

needed outcomes for the team, and set expectations for sharing information with the manager.

3. Ensure that each person feels a level of interaction safety, so they are willing and able to speak up and raise challenges, problems, and opportunities as needed.

4. Ask team members what they need to exercise their agency or increase their level of agency, including what organizational barriers block agency, and take steps to remove these barriers.

5. Identify and communicate the types of situations and decisions that need to be raised up to higher managerial levels for discussion and for attention. In this way, the individual and the team know where they have autonomy to make a decision and where others need to be included, either for broader gathering of information or for decision-making.

Seven Actions Managers Can Take to Unleash Agency for Themselves

Managers and supervisors need to not only support their direct reports and teams in exercising and claiming their agency, but also exercise agency in their own roles, rather than feeling squashed in the middle between their own manager and those who report to them. It is a challenge to navigate these two aspects of agency—enabling others to have it, and claiming it for themselves. In addition to the ways for individuals to unleash agency identified in Chapter 8, we offer more practices below that can enable managers to unleash agency for themselves, given their unique role:

1. Reflect on what it means to be a manager today and the shift that is needed in the role as they move to greater delegation, coordination, and support of their direct reports and others to exercise greater agency.

2. Assess where they are already exercising agency and where they could exercise more agency, if the conditions were right, and negotiate with their manager.

3. Consider where their agency would enhance organization success, bringing more of their voice and thinking to interactions and implementing actions.

4. Identify what they need to do their best work and encourage managers to have those conversations with their manager.

5. Discuss the learning objectives regarding agency as a manager with their team and with their manager as they move to greater agency.

6. Identify what work and activities they can let go of and what they need to incorporate as they shift their role to one of exercising greater agency.

7. Remember that they, too, are on a learning journey of change, and identify what support they need in this transition to greater agency for them and the people who report to them.

What Managers and Supervisors Gain

As managers and supervisors spend their time establishing boundaries and guardrails and improving delegation, they will free up time for the things that truly add value: time to see the bigger picture, coach and develop people, and think about improvements to the organization's functioning and efficiency. We have seen this happen in connection with meetings. In many organizations, people are overburdened with meetings, many of which lack focus, some of which might not be necessary. With greater agency, managers experiment with how to have more effective meetings by having the right people meet at the right time, to do the right work with the right tools. Others create thinking time by either reducing or eliminating some meetings. One organization asked people to cancel all standing meetings for two weeks and then reassessed which meetings were critical, who needed to be involved, and for how long. The payoff from freeing up time and energy are just some examples of how everybody wins when managers and supervisors exercise greater agency.

Chapter 11
Senior Leaders Getting Different

At the beginning of the transition toward agency, the leaders' role is to see the need for change, buy into the change effort, and communicate the "why" to the organization. At this later stage, their role is to support and live the new behavior and culture, advocate for it, and hold everyone in the organization accountable to it. This is not always easy. Assessment D in the resources section provides a self-assessment checklist for senior leaders to use as they lead through the change to a culture of agency.

Ceding Control

Over time, many leaders have learned that their role at the top is about control—creating consistency and controlling others—and they have bought into the understanding that, if you put in enough controls, nothing will go awry. However, when people in an organization have agency, leaders give up that control and, instead, trust their people. They accept that they do not have the answers to all the organization's challenges and need to include others in the decision-making process. As this happens, and as more decisions are made closest to the issues by those who have the relevant information and expertise, mistakes will be reduced, and leaders will be able to focus their attention where it is most needed.

For example, we have seen that when manufacturing organizations trust the frontline to exercise their agency—to solve problems and make decisions related to their work instead of pushing questions up a chain of command—quality goes up, errors go down, and the time to market improves. On the other hand, when the frontline does not have the ability to exercise agency, sometimes things do not go as well. Outside "experts" are often brought in who don't fully understand the local problem and often fail to consult or engage with people on the front line, who often have a greater understanding of the issue and ideas on how to address it. Not listening to the people who have the local knowledge creates waste, causes delay in addressing the problems, and brings down the morale of frontline people. The more senior leaders can understand this perspective and cede control in favor of unleashing agency throughout the organization, the more the potential for a higher-performing organization increases.

Supporting Agency

It is crucial that leaders set the tone at the top through demonstrating a deep personal commitment to the transformational process and the need for agency as a senior management team. They need to constantly repeat why agency is important both to the organization and to individual and team success, and they must model and enable behaviors that fully engage people to exercise their autonomy, authority, and leadership. As part of their role, senior leaders must find ways to celebrate and highlight examples of individuals, teams, and managers exercising agency in their everyday interactions and work.

One CEO we work with continuously looks for ways to say "yes" to decisions made or ideas proposed by members of the organization. He believes that the people he hired will have good ideas and that supporting their thinking encourages them to take risks and continue to add value to the organization.

> I start with "yes" because I know there will be aspects of the ideas that will move the organization forward. Although they might not be perfect or my way of solving a problem, I have trust in the ideas enough to know they will be directionally right.
>
> Rich Dewey,
> CEO, New York Independent
> System Operator

Additionally, he has boundaries and guardrails in place so that any wayward decisions made will not go too far off track. When he has enhancements to other people's ideas, he shares his thinking in ways that build upon, not dismiss, what team members have created. He believes that people need to know that they and their decisions are trusted, and to know that their work won't be discounted or reworked by their leader or manager. With this understanding, people are able to take his comments as supportive enhancements rather than criticism.

Creating a Learning Organization Where Agency Flourishes

Senior leaders need to create a learning organization as they move toward agency—a workplace in which there is an emphasis on continuous learning, adaptation, and innovation among its members. Such an environment requires each person, including senior leaders, to be open to new ideas and to enhance their interactions and professional skills. It involves diligently conducting after-action reviews to learn from situations and applying those lessons learned to future situations. Slowing down to review and learn can be a challenge for organizations that have an emphasis on the model of "go fast to go faster."

We had a client who told us they did not have the time to slow down to build a team and work on the quality of their interactions. Instead, they always jumped straight in to doing the work. When we asked if they ever needed to do rework or revisit decisions, they replied, "Yes, we do rework all the time!"—and then the light bulb went on.

It is crucial to bear in mind that it is impossible to have a learning organization *and* a high-punishment organization. Learning new ways of being, or trying out innovative ideas, will lead to failure, missteps, and mistakes. This is the nature of gaining knowledge and these failures are an opportunity for learning and trying other methods. However, when something goes wrong, many organizations turn to blame. Some organizations ask the "Five Whos?"—Who did it? Who did it? Who did it? Who did it? Who did it?—they just want to identify who is to blame! This approach does not identify the root cause of the problems or fully understand or resolve them, as considering the "Five Whys?" would. Instead, it spreads resentment and distrust throughout an organization and makes people risk-averse and leery of making problems visible or trying new things. In short, this binary of guilt or innocence torpedoes a learning environment and is a huge impediment to unleashing agency.

When leaders communicate the benefits of agency for the organization and give it their full support over time, they must also acknowledge that people, including themselves, are on a learning curve—and that is okay. Everything will not run perfectly or smoothly. Mistakes will be made as part of the change process, and they need to be seen as opportunities to learn, develop, and grow, as openings to teach people how better to exercise agency and not go back to the way things were.

The bottom line for senior leaders is *leaders must believe they have the right people with the competencies needed to excel in their areas of responsibility.* One of our reviewers for this book, Kathy Scheiern, shared her experience with agency and the devastating impact of leaders not trusting their people:

> As an upper-level manager of a Fortune 500 company (long ago), I attempted to implement many of the steps outlined in this book because I believed in and trusted the people in my department. We existed in a somewhat isolated environment, so it worked well for a long time. But any attempt on my part to share that process with the rest of the organization was met with very firm resistance—not by the rank and file who really wanted change, but by the other senior managers who were completely unwilling to change, in part because they didn't really trust their people.

Many leaders need to adopt a new style and form of leadership that enables people in the organization to learn and experiment within their role and authority. Ultimately, leaders need to be willing to let go of control, trust their people, give them the benefit of the doubt, and let them do the job they were hired to do. If leaders and organizations stay focused on their mission, vision, and values, and trust their people, they can't go too far astray.

Chapter 12
Human Resource Systems and Management Practices

In this chapter, we look at the ways that human resource systems and management practices will need to change as organizations move to a culture of agency. We build upon discussions begun in Chapters 6 and 7 as part of the process to agency in organizations (Step 8: clarify manager and direct report responsibilities; Step 9: reassess and enhance HR systems; and Step 10: monitor progress and refine strategy) and elaborate on how the new culture needs to be supported through human resource systems and management practices. In many ways, the client for human resource functions is the organization itself and the desired agency culture change. As agency is unleashed, human resource systems and processes need to be updated and enhanced to reflect the organization's new culture and practices. With the creation of the new narrative, as changing mindsets and behaviors become the norm, and the organization moves to the TO state, organizational systems and processes will need to integrate agency as a critical component of how the organization operates. Assessment E provides a way for Human Resources to measure the organization's progress as it undertakes these changes. Enhancements will be needed in the following areas:

Job Descriptions and Performance Management Must Align with New Expectations

Agency needs to be incorporated by Human Resources into all job descriptions and needs to be a key part of performance feedback so people at all levels know what is expected of them.

Job descriptions need to clearly state the following:

▶ Where an individual has autonomy and is able to make decisions.

▶ Expectations for goals and outcomes.

▶ How each person's role connects to the larger organizational mission, vision, and/or strategic direction.

▶ Protocols for when and how people need to bring their manager or supervisor into decisions or when to share critical information with them.

▶ That managers may need an initial period of increased interaction with a new hire or a new team to calibrate and support the individual's or team's ability to exercise agency and leadership in their role.

▶ The boundaries of a person's role should be clearly identified when contracting with managers and supervisors.

Job descriptions need to include agency-centric language such as "takes initiative," "self-starter," "responsible for," "develops expertise in," "willingness to speak up and share ideas," "ability to collaborate and act independently," as well as the words "authority," "autonomy," and "leadership," as relevant.

Managers need to incorporate elements of agency, including goal setting and feedback, into performance management. Agency needs to be at the forefront of performance conversations. There needs to be goal setting for individuals, which includes focus on the role agency can play. Individuals will be evaluated on how they exercise agency within their role, and within and across teams. Discussions need to include how people will benefit from further education or coaching around agency.

Performance discussions, regular feedback, and check-ins become a required part of the process. These discussions or check-ins will involve ensuring that managers are removing barriers that might limit people in exercising their agency, as well as providing the tools and resources needed for higher performance.

Once the culture of agency has been established, expectations have been communicated both to current and new employees, and everyone has had the training, clarity, and support about the exercise of agency, along with the necessary interaction safety, then agency will become a standard performance expectation, as organizations start to view agency as critical to their success. It will become a requirement of employment similar to ensuring safety or carrying out other job responsibilities. When not performed properly, even after the provision of additional coaching and support, a lack of exercising of agency will be grounds for termination because the person is not supporting the mindsets and behaviors needed of each person. However, it is imperative that a culture of agency, and all that that entails, is in place first.

Enhancing Criteria: Hiring and Promotions

Hiring

Hiring criteria need to make clear that there is an expectation that all new hires will exercise agency in their role. This means all job announcements state that the organization is seeking individuals who are:

▶ willing and able to take initiative, work with autonomy, make decisions, and take leadership in their interactions and work responsibilities

▶ willing to speak up and share their ideas and opinions

▶ able to work effectively in a team to collaborate, share information, and accomplish goals with others

▶ willing to effectively address and work through conflict

▶ able to engage with diversity of thought, perspectives, and experiences

Promotion

The criteria for promotion seeks out people who:

▶ demonstrate agency in their work

▶ demonstrate agency while working with teams

▶ assist others in exercising agency

▶ contribute to a culture in which agency is nourished

For managers and supervisors, the additional criteria for promotion would include:

- creating an inclusive and trusting environment

- supporting, managing, and coaching people to exercise greater agency

- removing barriers that limit people's ability to do their best work

- demonstrating agency in their own work

It is imperative that the new criteria are communicated clearly and frequently. Organizations, however, need to expect some growing pains and turnover as change happens. When one organization made a similar culture change and shifted its promotion criteria, they found some leaders were technically competent but did not demonstrate the skills needed to create the new culture. When these leaders were not promoted, they were quite surprised. Organizations may expect a similar response as they move to greater agency and include agency in their promotion criteria.

Enhancing Development Opportunities to Learn and Grow

For many organizations, moving to agency will represent a major learning curve. Ongoing education and processes that assist individuals, managers, and leaders to learn more about how to exercise agency are critical to the organization's successful use of agency. These might include the following methods.

- The creation of both formal and informal feedback processes to support and encourage people to make decisions, enhance their communication and information sharing, and build trusting partnerships.

▶ The use of synchronous and asynchronous learning experiences to further people's skill development and their understanding of how to exercise greater agency.

▶ The provision of agency coaches and/or Human Resources staff to provide feedback to individuals and teams to deepen their skills and abilities and identify examples of agency in action.

▶ Holding Q&A sessions to educate and further develop understanding and practice of agency.

Embedding Agency into Recognition and Rewards and Sharing Stories of Success

To address the challenges of skepticism around whether agency is possible, or if others are truly exercising agency, recognition and rewards systems incorporate the exercise of agency as a key element. This can be achieved through the following measures.

▶ Ensuring individuals, teams, and managers/supervisors are recognized and rewarded for both their contributions and their exercise of agency in accomplishing them, so as to make agency visible to the organization as a model of success.

▶ Sharing individual and team success stories to bring life to the new narrative and show examples of how people are indeed moving into that new narrative with agency.

An example of a success story is the way that at one organization making agency a way of life has resulted in leaders reducing their micromanagement of people, which allows individuals and teams to make their own decisions and act more rapidly. In turn, with greater agency, people there feel the freedom to work on what is most important and are more willing to collaborate and rally to support others within their areas and across the organization.

Or, in another organization leading with agency, two managers got together and created a plan to merge their areas to create greater efficiencies and reduce wasted effort. The two managers decided which of them would lead the function and which would report to that person. Together they went to the vice president with the proposed merger and their identified new roles.

Stories like these help others see how agency can make a positive difference—and that it is safe for them to embrace agency, too.

► Creating an organization-wide award for individuals and teams who demonstrate the new culture in their work. In one organization, people were able to nominate individuals, teams, and managers who were displaying the new mindsets and behaviors. Everyone nominated was acknowledged with a certificate of appreciation and two or three of the nominees received greater recognition and a cash award. In another organization, in the beginning stages of their effort, people were encouraged to give others a card which said "Thanks for stepping up. You make a difference." People gladly posted those cards in their cubicles or offices and felt seen, acknowledged, and encouraged to do more.

Measuring What Matters

It is critical that the organization focuses on the measures that matter to demonstrate the payoff of exercising agency. These measures will be different for each organization, but may include enhancements in:

- ▶ quality
- ▶ customer service
- ▶ innovation
- ▶ decision making
- ▶ physical and interaction safety
- ▶ problem solving
- ▶ employee well-being
- ▶ job satisfaction

These elements all demonstrate the return on investment that greater agency provides. Most important is identifying the measures that matter to the organization itself and are tracked and reported on a regular basis. For some organizations this might be customer service or quality, whereas for others it might be safety. One of our clients needed to dramatically reduce their cost per unit. With the introduction of agency, people were able to make individual and group decisions, both small and large, about how they could reduce production costs in their areas of responsibility. This avoided negative impacts to operations, layoffs, or other typical cost reduction methods. With decisions being made locally, closer to the problem, and in partnership with others, the organization found process improvements that enabled them to achieve their goal. Cost reduction was a measure that mattered to the organization's financial success and greater agency led them to it; and in the process, they reaped benefits far beyond cost reduction.

Conclusion

Where Do I Start and What's Around the Corner?

Where Do I Start?

We hope this book has spurred your thinking and excitement about bringing greater agency to your work life and your organization. More and more we are hearing commentators in the media talking about the need for individuals to have greater agency in their lives. Now the opportunity is for organizations to also understand how agency for everyone at every level can transform the organization, its performance, and its workforce.

We have shared the multiple ways to start on this journey—how to change the culture from an organizational view and how individuals, teams, managers, and senior leaders can take action to unleash and exercise agency to make it a way of organizational life for everyone. We understand this is a journey of change, courage, experimentation, and learning, and we hope it is one you and your organization will take. Enhancing our organizations is vital to even higher performance and long-term success.

One place to start is by discussing what agency is, and why it is important for you and your organization. The assessments are a useful beginning to identify some of the gaps that may exist and to enable a dialogue with people in the organization about the opportunities and enhancements possible if greater agency were present. But it is not an easy transition. The move to greater agency takes leaning into discomfort, and the willingness to speak up.[18] It takes listening to others as allies and inviting other perspectives and street corners. We know some of you are already demonstrating aspects of agency in your work interactions—sharing that with and encouraging others to exercise their agency will create a ripple effect and a collective voice for the need for change.

Around the Corner

As we look to the future, we believe agency will be even more important as artificial intelligence (AI) becomes more embedded in our everyday experiences, interactions, and ways of working. If the human workforce is to leverage and collaborate with AI, we will need to tap into our skills that set us apart. This requires bringing our thinking, empathy, creativity, discernment, and hopes for a better tomorrow for humankind to how things are done.

We are already seeing how ChatGPT and other forms of generative AI technology are transforming many tasks—from taking notes in a meeting, to creating trip itineraries, to writing papers and books, to serving as a companion. We believe agency will help us take the leap forward in utilizing those technologies alongside our full capabilities and potential. Just as we must stay open to learning from AI and technology, we must cultivate greater agency—authority, autonomy, and leadership—to bring our best selves to today and to the future.

Your Challenge

The journey to greater agency and higher performance is before us. We would love to hear about your experiences and learning along the way. Share your thoughts with us at: kjcg.com/the-power-of-agency or by emailing us at: kjcg411@kjcg.com.

As we said in our book *Be BIG*, it is time for every one of us to step up, step out, and be BOLD. Agency is a fundamental part of doing that. We wish you all the best in your journey of change. In most organizations, some people already have agency, but the breakthrough is when everyone has agency. Agency is needed more than ever. And it is needed NOW!

Notes

Preface

1. Yabome Gilpin-Jackson, "Participant Experiences of Transformational Change in Large-Scale Organization Development Interventions (LODIs)," *Leadership & Organization Development Journal* 38, no. 3 (May 2, 2017): 419–32. https://doi.org/10.1108/lodj-12-2015-0284.

2. Bradley J. Hastings and Gavin M. Schwarz, "Leading Change Processes for Success: A Dynamic Application of Diagnostic and Dialogic Organization Development," *The Journal of Applied Behavioral Science* 58, no. 1 (May 29, 2021): 120–48. https://doi.org/10.1177/00218863211019561.

3. Frederick A. Miller, Monica E. Biggs, and Judith H. Katz, *Change Champions: A Dialogic Approach to Creating an Inclusive Culture* (North Vancouver: BMI, 2022).

4. A. Eteläpelto, K. Vähäsantanen, P. Hökkä, and S. Paloniemi, "What Is Agency? Conceptualizing Professional Agency at Work." *Educational Research Review* 10 (2013): 45–65. https://doi.org/10.1016/j.edurev.2013.05.001.

Chapter 1

5. We first heard the term GET DIFFERENT in this context used by John Bader, a senior leader, as the basis of a significant organization-wide change he was implementing. People were reminded every day of the need to get different through journals they were asked to keep, education sessions in which people had "knee to knee" conversations to share more deeply and honestly with one another, and even wrist bracelets with "GET DIFFERENT" on them.

6. Yves Van Durme et al., "Deloitte 2023 Global Human Capital Trends," *Deloitte Insights*, February 2, 2023. https://www2.deloitte.com/us/en/insights/focus/human-capital-trends/2023/future-of-workforce-management.html.

7. As early as 2001, Daniel Pink was describing workers as "free agents." Daniel H. Pink, *Free Agent Nation: How America's New Independent Workers Are Transforming the Way We Live* (New York: Grand Central Publishing, 2001). For a more recent discussion see Mark C. Perna, "3 Ways Employers Can Win Over the Free Agent Workforce," *Forbes*, April 20, 2023. https://www.forbes.com/sites/markcperna/2023/04/20/3-ways-employers-can-win-over-the-free-agent-workforce/?sh=2fec04ff4a18.

8. Debra Sabatini Hennelly and Bradley Schurman, "Bridging Generational Divides in Your Workplace," *Harvard*

Business Review, January 10, 2023. https://hbr.org/2023 /01/bridging-generational-divides-in-your-workplace.

Chapter 3

9. See Frederick A. Miller and Judith H. Katz, "Moving Inclusion Along the Path to Agency," *Organizational Development Review* 55, no. 2 (2023): 50–56, in which we discuss the developmental process of moving organizations along the path from a monocultural club to one that is inclusive and supports agency at every level.

10. See Frederick A. Miller and Judith H. Katz, *Safe Enough to Soar: Accelerating Trust, Inclusion, & Collaboration in the Workplace* (San Francisco: Berrett-Koehler Publishers, 2018), for a more detailed discussion of interaction safety.

11. From Verna Myers, a leading diversity and inclusion expert.

12. Amy Waczek, "Semco—Insanity That Works," *Epic Work Epic Life*, May 14, 2021 (blog). https://epicworkepiclife.com /semco-insanity-that-works/. This is an update from the original article by Ricardo Semler, "Managing Without Managers," *Harvard Business Review*, September–October 1989, in which Semler discussed the Semco journey, philosophy, structure, and outcomes of their workplace culture.

Part II

13. For more information about Dialogic Organization Development, see Gervase R. Bushe and Robert J. Marshak, *Dialogic Organization Development: The Theory and Practice of Transformational Change* (San Francisco: Berrett-Koehler Publishers, 2015).

Chapter 5

14. Letian Zhang, "The Changing Role of Managers," *Social Science Research Network*, January 1, 2020. https://doi.org /10.2139/ssrn.3877673.

Chapter 6

15. Frederick A. Miller, Monica E. Biggs, and Judith H. Katz, *Change Champions: A Dialogic Approach to Creating an Inclusive Culture* (North Vancouver: BMI, 2022).

16. For a fuller discussion of change management, see Scott Keller and Bill Schaninger, *Beyond Performance 2.0: A Proven Approach to Leading Large-Scale Change* (New York: John Wiley & Sons, 2019).

17. For a more in-depth discussion of the Leadership feedback pods see Judith H. Katz, "Grow Yourself, Grow Your Team, Grow Your Business: The Challenge for Today's Leaders," *Practising Social Change*: *NTL Institute for Applied Behavioural Science* 4 (November 2011): 17–20.

Conclusion

18. Judith H. Katz and Frederick A. Miller, *Opening Doors to Teamwork and Collaboration: 4 Keys That Change Everything* (San Francisco: Berrett-Koehler Publishers, 2013).

Agency Resources:
Assessments

A. Individuals

B. Teams

C. Managers and Supervisors

D. Senior Leaders

E. Human Resource Systems and Management Practices

In this section we have included five assessments to enable people to calibrate the extent to which they are exercising agency and, depending upon their scores, identify areas in which they might want to further develop and grow. Many different mindsets and behaviors add up to the ability to exercise agency. As you complete an assessment, it is helpful to pay attention to those items in which you are doing well and have the ability to exercise agency, and those areas that need further attention and improvement.

Our suggestion is for each person to fill out the appropriate assessment(s) individually and then to share the assessment with a team member, manager, or someone who can provide additional feedback and insights. In particular, you may want to identify those areas that score less than 6 (on a 10-point scale) and discuss ways you and others could move that score higher.

People may complete more than one assessment. For example, an individual might complete the individual assessment as well as the team assessment. Similarly, a manager or supervisor might fill out both the manager assessment to identify how well they are supporting unleashing agency for their direct reports, as well as complete the individual assessment to see the extent to which they feel they have agency as an individual. A Human Resources professional might explore their own experience of agency in completing the individual assessment and then the HR Systems and Management Practices assessment to examine the extent to which the organization itself is providing the support that people at all levels need for greater agency.

Having discussions with others is an important part of completing these assessments as they can provide helpful feedback, support, and possible actions to move to greater agency.

A. Agency Self-Assessment for Individuals

The following self-assessment allows individuals to calibrate the extent to which they are exercising agency. It is useful for people to fill out the form by themselves and reflect on areas of competency and areas for continuous improvement. The individual may want to share learning or takeaways from the assessment with colleagues and/or their manager.

An 8 and above is a strong "yes" and indicates that that particular behavior or mindset is being practiced by the respondent. For a score of 7, small changes might be needed to move to a higher score. Any items that are 6 or below are important to address and to develop an improvement strategy for them.

For each question, assess yourself on a 0–10 scale.

0 being not at all————10 being to a great extent

Individual Self-Assessment

Question	Score (0-10)
1. I understand how my work connects to the organization's vision, mission, and strategic direction.	
2. I have clarity about the *boundaries* of my work (i.e., the scope of my work and where I have authority to make decisions).	
3. I have clarity about the *responsibilities* of my work.	
4. I have clarity about the *outcomes* of my work.	
5. I have clarity about the *timelines* of my work.	
6. I have the autonomy I need to make decisions.	
7. I have the autonomy and authority needed to accomplish my job.	
8. I am trusted by my manager to make the decisions we have agreed are mine to make.	
9. I can use my know-how, skills, thinking, and experience to accomplish my job.	
10. My manager understands what I need to exercise agency.	
11. My manager removes obstacles and barriers that block my ability to exercise agency.	
12. I am able to innovate and solve problems in my areas of responsibility.	
13. Information I need to do my job flows freely from all sources (manager, team members, direct reports, people on other teams, and the organization as a whole).	

(continued)

Individual Self-Assessment (*continued*)

Question	Score (0-10)
14. I am transparent about my decision-making process and share not only my decisions but how I arrived at them, when that is helpful.	
15. I am able to contribute my ideas that align with my knowledge, but may be outside of my role and responsibility, in order to improve the overall organization.	
16. My manager hears and acts on my contributions and suggestions.	
17. I experience an environment of interaction safety, with the ability to speak up and raise tough issues when needed.	
18. When I see something is misaligned, I address it directly with all involved parties, whether teammates, leaders, or outside my team.	
19. If I make a mistake, I know it will be supported by others as a learning opportunity.	
20. I frequently solicit other people's thoughts, knowing that there are other possible solutions.	
21. I have opportunities to grow and expand my skills and knowledge.	
22. I am recognized and rewarded by my manager, teammates, and others for exercising agency.	
23. My manager is considerate of my work-life-me goals as we plan projects and timelines.	

B. Agency Self-Assessment for Teams

The following self-assessment allows teams to calibrate the extent to which they are exercising agency. It is useful for each person to fill out the form individually, reflecting on areas of competency and areas for continuous improvement, and then have a team dialogue about each person's answers. The team may want to share learning or takeaways from the assessment with their manager, as appropriate.

A score of 8 and above is a strong "yes" and indicates that the behavior or mindset being measured is being practiced by the team. For a score of 7, small changes might be needed to move to a higher score. Any items that score 6 or below are important to address and to develop an improvement strategy for them.

For each question, assess how the team operates on a 0–10 scale.

0 being not at all————10 being to a great extent

Team Self-Assessment

Question	Score (0-10)
1. We are clear about how our work connects to the organization's vision, mission, and/or strategic direction.	
2. We have clarity about the *boundaries* of our work as a team (i.e., the scope of our work and where we have the authority to make decisions).	
3. We have clarity about the *responsibilities* of our work as a team.	
4. We have clarity about the *outcomes* of our work as a team.	
5. We have clarity about the *timelines* of our work as a team.	
6. We have the autonomy we need to make team decisions.	
7. We have clarity about where we work independently and interdependently as a team.	
8. We are trusted to make decisions by the manager accountable for the project.	
9. We have clarity about how we will make decisions.	
10. We have productive collaboration.	
11. We solve problems effectively.	
12. The manager accountable for the project understands what we need to exercise agency.	

Team Self-Assessment (*continued*)

Question	Score (0-10)
13. The manager accountable for the project removes obstacles or barriers so that we can do our best work.	
14. The manager accountable for the project provides the tools, resources, and access we need to accomplish our goals.	
15. We have an environment of interaction safety, with the ability to speak up and raise issues when needed.	
16. When we see something is misaligned, or have a misunderstanding or disagreement, we address it directly with one another.	
17. When someone makes a mistake, we use it as a learning opportunity rather than punish them.	
18. We celebrate and recognize our individual and team accomplishments.	
19. We are mindful of one another's workload and work-life-me needs.	

C. Agency Self-Assessment for Managers and Supervisors

The following self-assessment allows managers or supervisors to calibrate the extent to which they are exercising agency. The manager or supervisor may want to share learning or takeaways from the assessment with their manager, as appropriate.

An 8 and above score is a strong "yes" and indicates that the behavior or mindset that's being measured is being practiced by the manager or supervisor. For a score of 7, small changes might be needed to move to a higher score. Any items that score 6 or below are important to address and to develop an improvement strategy for them.

For each question, assess yourself on a 0–10 scale.

0 being not at all————10 being to a great extent

Manager and Supervisor Self-Asessement

Question	Score (0-10)
1. I ensure team members understand how their work connects to the organization's vision, mission, and/ or strategic direction.	
2. I provide clarity about *boundaries* (i.e., their scope of work and where people can make decisions).	
3. I provide clarity about *responsibilities*.	
4. I provide clarity of *outcomes*.	
5. I provide clarity of *timelines*.	
6. I remove barriers and obstacles that might limit people's ability to exercise agency.	
7. I trust people to make decisions at the right level.	
8. People are clear about the types of decisions that need to be discussed at higher levels in the organization.	
9. I am transparent about my decision-making process and share not only my decisions but how I arrived at them.	
10. I frequently solicit other people's input, knowing that there are other possible solutions.	
11. I foster an environment of interaction safety with people in which they feel the freedom to speak up and raise issues and opportunities with me.	
12. When someone on my team makes a mistake, I take the opportunity to use it as a learning experience.	

(continued)

Manager and Supervisor Self-Asessement
(*continued*)

Question	Score (0-10)
13. I ask team members what they need to increase their ability to exercise greater agency.	
14. I seek out opportunities for team members to develop their skills and grow.	
15. I ask team members for feedback about my support of their agency.	
16. I recognize and reward team members who demonstrate agency.	
17. I have more time to coach, manage, and give feedback to team members as a result of supporting their agency.	
18. I discuss with each team member their work-life-me integration as we plan projects and timelines.	

D. Agency Self-Assessment for Senior Leaders

The following self-assessment allows senior leaders to calibrate the extent to which they are exercising agency. A senior leader may want to share learning or takeaways from the assessment with their peers and/ or direct reports. A CEO might want to share their findings with the chair of the board.

A score of 8 and above is a strong "yes" and indicates that the behavior or mindset that's being measured is being practiced by the senior leader. For a score of 7, small changes might be needed to move to a higher score. Any items that score 6 or below are important to address and to develop an improvement strategy for them.

For each question respond on a 0–10 scale.

0 being not at all————10 being to a great extent

Senior Leader Self-Assessment

Question	Score (0-10)
1. We have created a compelling FROM→TO culture vision.	
2. We have created an enhanced organization narrative that includes why agency is critical to higher individual, team, and organization performance.	
3. We are committed to creating a culture of agency.	
4. We demonstrate our commitment to creating a culture of agency by ensuring adequate resources and training are provided to effectively implement agency.	
5. We invest our time as leaders to ensure that agency permeates the organization.	
6. We communicate frequently, as individuals and as a senior leadership team, why agency is important for the organization and for each person's ability to do their best work.	
7. We inform people of the progress of our work in creating a culture of agency, discuss the next steps, and ask for feedback and ideas on how to improve our efforts.	
8. As a leadership team, we model the new mindsets and behaviors that support everyone's ability to exercise greater agency.	
9. We look for signs of success, and reward and acknowledge people's exercise of agency to communicate examples of agency in action.	
10. We are adapting our leadership styles to enable people to exercise greater agency.	

Senior Leader Self-Assessment (*continued*)

Question	Score (0-10)
11. We support people throughout the organization to make the right decisions at their level.	
12. When someone makes a mistake, we take it as an opportunity to learn.	
13. As a senior leadership team, we are fostering an environment of interaction safety in which people feel the freedom to speak up and raise tough issues.	
14. We are mindful and respectful of people's work-life-me integration as we plan projects and timelines.	

E. Agency Assessment for Human Resource Systems and Management Practices

The following provides an assessment of Human Resource (HR) Systems and Management Practices to calibrate the extent to which these systems and processes are promoting agency in the structure and culture of the organization. This assessment can be taken by HR and/or senior leaders. It may be useful to have both member(s) of HR and senior leaders take the assessment separately and then discuss their scores as a group and identify actions to move up the scale and/or to address disparities in how they see the organization.

Any item scoring 8 and above is a strong "yes" and indicates that the policy or behavior being measured is being implemented in the organization. For a score of 7, small changes might be needed to move to a higher score. Any items that score 6 or below are important to address and to develop an improvement strategy for them.

For each question respond on a 0–10 scale.

0 being not at all————10 being to a great extent

Human Resource Systems

Question	Score (0-10)
1. Job descriptions include the exercise of agency.	
2. Hiring criteria include an expectation that new hires will exercise agency.	
3. Onboarding processes include content about agency and the mindsets and behaviors that are needed from individuals to exercise agency.	
4. Promotion criteria ensure that individuals demonstrate agency.	
5. Promotion criteria ensure managers nourish people's ability to exercise agency.	
6. There are formal feedback processes in place to support people's ability to exercise agency.	
7. The organization provides educational and development opportunities for all members to grow and develop new skills to support and exercise agency.	
8. Coaches are available to support individuals and teams in deepening their skills and abilities to exercise agency.	
9. Change management resources are in place to monitor and assess progress, and to support the change effort.	
10. Leaders and managers are rewarded and recognized for modeling the new behaviors and mindsets that support everyone's ability to exercise greater agency.	

(continued)

Human Resource Systems (*continued*)

Question	Score (0-10)
11. Success stories of how people are using agency to accomplish their goals, individually and in teams, are shared throughout the organization.	
12. The organization communicates the importance and meaning of agency across the organization through town hall meetings, electronic bulletin boards, internal messaging systems, newsletters, website, etc.	
13. People's morale and well-being are increasing as a result of creating a culture of agency.	
14. Our performance metrics are improving as a result of creating a culture of agency (customer satisfaction, quality, safety, time to market, interactions with clients/customers, etc.).	

Management Practices

Question	Score (0-10)
1. Our management systems support a culture of agency.	
2. Managers meet with new hires during their integration process to discuss the importance of modeling behaviors and mindsets that enable agency.	
3. Managers discuss with their direct reports how their role connects to the organization's mission, vision, values, and strategic direction.	
4. Managers hold regular check-in meetings with people to hear what barriers and obstacles they are experiencing and what tools, resources, and access they need to do their best work.	
5. Managers coach, develop, and provide feedback to people to enable them to grow and exercise greater agency.	
6. Managers recognize and reward people for exercising agency.	

Acknowledgments

POWER OF AGENCY

First, we want to thank Dan Ross, SVP & CHRO at Day and Zimmermann, because although we had heard people talking about agency, when you said it and applied it to your organization, something clicked and this book was born. Thank you, Dan; we are in your debt.

Thank you Véronique Wendolovske, of The Kaleel Jamison Consulting Group, Inc., for your patience in shepherding us through this process, especially as you completed your final months of pregnancy. Your patience with us, and your commitment to tracking all the details, made this book possible.

Thanks to Yabome Gilpin-Jackson and Chris Del Vecchio for your wonderful forewords. You inspire us! We are so glad to know and work with you. And, thanks to those who wrote endorsements for the back cover: Gervase Bushe, Rich Dewey, Bob Marshak, Sushma Sharma, Wendi Williams; thanks for your kind words about the book. We have known you for a while and greatly appreciate who you are and what you give to organizations.

Thank you Monica Biggs and Kathy Clements for your early reading and feedback while the book was in its initial stages. Your insight and thoughtful critique helped elevate the book from the very beginning.

Thank you Lindsey Tate for your expertise and partnership in helping us organize and re-organize the book. You helped make the reading of the book so much easier for everyone. Jeevan Sivasubramaniam, your/our Bean People always give a signature touch to our books. Everyone loves the jumping Bean Person when you turn the pages fast. Thanks, Amoreena O'Bryon for your work on the cover and making the charts work. Thanks to Kate Richmond and Bill Yoh; you were the last to read the manuscript, you gave it that last special touch by adding your insights. And thanks to all those we polled about the title and the front and back covers . . . you, too, made a difference.

A special shout out to our client and friends at the Jacksonville Zoo and Gardens, Jeff Ettling, Paula Shields, Tom Cornwell, Eric Turner, and the wonderful team members for letting us test the agency concept and the questionnaires. You, too, gave us the confidence to pursue the concept and this book.

Thanks to The Kaleel Jamison Consulting Group, Inc., Troy Hub members, especially Tara Whittle, for your thinking and editing, and for asking great questions; your touch always makes something better; and to Alison VanDerVolgen for your meticulous reading, editing of the manuscript, and believing in the book. Tara and Alison, we are in your debt once again. Finally, thank you to Amadi Turner-Tarver for picking up the mantel and getting us across the finish line during Véronique's parental leave.

As always, a thanks to our marriage partners, Pauline Kamen Miller and David Levine; once again, you have been patient with us and added tremendous value through your comments about the book and, more importantly, your love and support enabled us to dedicate so much time to the project.

Finally, a big thank you to our friends and partners at our publisher, Berrett-Koehler—you are so wonderful, thoughtful, and caring to us as authors and as people. We are proud to publish our fifth book with you. A special thanks to Steve Piersanti for once again seeing that we had something to say and encouraging us throughout this process. Again, thanks to Jeevan and team for accepting our book outline and saying, "go for it!" Thank you, Ashley Ingram, for your assistance, especially with the cover; your wisdom and experience helped us create one that we really like. And, thanks to Justine Buchanan and Angela Piliouras for your guidance in editing and production. It takes a village, and we are so grateful to everyone who has shared their wisdom and insights with us along the way to making this book a reality!

Index

Note: Page numbers followed by *t* indicate tables; page numbers followed by *f* indicate figures; page numbers followed by n indicate notes.

About the Authors

Frederick A. Miller and Judith H. Katz

For more than fifty years, Fred and Judith have been working individually and together on organization and cultural transformation to create more inclusive and higher performing workplaces.

They started their business partnership in 1985. Fred left a management position at Connecticut General Life Insurance Company in the 1970s and first joined Kaleel Jamison in 1979. Judith then joined Fred in 1985 from faculty positions at the University of Oklahoma and San Diego State. It was a major turning point in both their lives.

As, CEO and Executive Vice President, Emeritus, respectively, for The Kaleel Jamison Consulting Group, Inc.—one of *Consulting Magazine's* Seven Small Jewels—Fred and Judith have partnered with hundreds of Fortune 100, and other companies, universities, governmental agencies, municipalities, and nonprofit organizations. Their aim is always to create organizations in which the level of interaction safety elevates the quality of interactions, leverages people's differences, and transforms workplaces into growth and learning environments where people's talents are unleashed, results are accelerated, and productivity soars. Their partnership is proof that teamwork and collaboration do create breakthroughs.

Through their thought leadership and practical approaches for transforming workplaces, they have brought their unique perspectives, passion, and energy, that few can match, to make a difference in organizations.

Together they have co-authored and co-edited seven books and hundreds of articles. Among their books is the groundbreaking *The Inclusion Breakthrough: Unleashing the Real Power of Diversity* (2002), the first book to address the need for inclusion in organizations and how to make systemic change.

Judith and Fred have each been honored with many of their field's most distinguished awards. In 2007, *Profiles in Diversity Journal* named them two of forty Pioneers of Diversity and in 2012, they were both honored as Legends of Diversity by the International Society of Diversity and Inclusion Professionals. Among other awards they have received are Fred's Lifetime Achievement Award and Service to the Network Award, presented by the Organization Development Network (ODN), and the Winds of Change Award from the Forum on Workplace Inclusion. More recently, Fred was the recipient of the NAACP Berkshires Branch WEB DuBois Award. Judith has received ODN's Lifetime Achievement Award, the Outstanding Achievement in Global Work Award, and the award for Communicating Organizational Development Knowledge, as well as the Cultural Competency Award from Diversity Training University International. Fred served in the United States Army, on Ben & Jerry's corporate board and Sage Colleges Board of Trustees, and currently serves on Day & Zimmermann's corporate board. Judith is Trustee Emerit on the Fielding Graduate University Board of Trustees where she served as a member, and served on Social Venture Network's and National Training Laboratories Institute's boards, as well as on the University of Massachusetts Dean's Leadership Council.

Their consulting practice, workshops, and conference presentations have impacted clients and groups around the globe.

Judith loves fishing and traveling with David, her husband.

Fred is a workaholic who loves being at home with his marriage partner, Pauline, and the fancy guppies that he raises.

Judith's extraversion and Fred's introversion often cause them to see the world from different street corners, which has led to many intense conversations, personal and professional revelations—and a lot of laughter and creativity.

Through their work together, they have been able, individually and collectively, to soar—and to inspire and enable individuals, teams, and organizations to do the same.

Berrett–Koehler
BK Publishers

Berrett-Koehler is an independent publisher dedicated to an ambitious mission: *Connecting people and ideas to create a world that works for all.*

Our publications span many formats, including print, digital, audio, and video. We also offer online resources, training, and gatherings. And we will continue expanding our products and services to advance our mission.

We believe that the solutions to the world's problems will come from all of us, working at all levels: in our society, in our organizations, and in our own lives. Our publications and resources offer pathways to creating a more just, equitable, and sustainable society. They help people make their organizations more humane, democratic, diverse, and effective (and we don't think there's any contradiction there). And they guide people in creating positive change in their own lives and aligning their personal practices with their aspirations for a better world.

And we strive to practice what we preach through what we call "The BK Way." At the core of this approach is *stewardship,* a deep sense of responsibility to administer the company for the benefit of all of our stakeholder groups, including authors, customers, employees, investors, service providers, sales partners, and the communities and environment around us. Everything we do is built around stewardship and our other core values of *quality, partnership, inclusion,* and *sustainability.*

This is why Berrett-Koehler is the first book publishing company to be both a B Corporation (a rigorous certification) and a benefit corporation (a for-profit legal status), which together require us to adhere to the highest standards for corporate, social, and environmental performance. And it is why we have instituted many pioneering practices (which you can learn about at www.bkconnection.com), including the Berrett-Koehler Constitution, the Bill of Rights and Responsibilities for BK Authors, and our unique Author Days.

We are grateful to our readers, authors, and other friends who are supporting our mission. We ask you to share with us examples of how BK publications and resources are making a difference in your lives, organizations, and communities at www.bkconnection.com/impact.

Dear reader,

Thank you for picking up this book and welcome to the worldwide BK community! You're joining a special group of people who have come together to create positive change in their lives, organizations, and communities.

What's BK all about?

Our mission is to connect people and ideas to create a world that works for all.

Why? Our communities, organizations, and lives get bogged down by old paradigms of self-interest, exclusion, hierarchy, and privilege. But we believe that can change. That's why we seek the leading experts on these challenges—and share their actionable ideas with you.

A welcome gift

To help you get started, we'd like to offer you a free copy of one of our bestselling ebooks:

www.bkconnection.com/welcome

When you claim your **free ebook,** you'll also be subscribed to our blog.

Our freshest insights

Access the best new tools and ideas for leaders at all levels on our blog at ideas.bkconnection.com.

Sincerely,
Your friends at Berrett-Koehler